EMIGRATION TO OTHER STATES
FROM
SOUTHSIDE VIRGINIA
VOLUME II

COMPILED
BY
KATHERINE B. ELLIOTT
SOUTH HILL
VIRGINIA

Please direct all correspondence and orders to:

www.southernhistoricalpress.com
or
SOUTHERN HISTORICAL PRESS, Inc.
PO BOX 1267
375 West Broad Street
Greenville, SC   29601
southernhistoricalpress@gmail.com

ISBN #0-89308-366-6

Printed in the United States of America

FOREWORD

The primary problem of people in other states with Virginia ancestry has been to establish when their ancestors left Virginia, and to what place they first migrated. This has been a problem to Virginia genealogical researchers, also, for many of these people sold out and disappeared from the county records with no indication of their ultimate destination.

As new territory was opened to settlement, or new counties formed, many of the settlers were on the move again. The lure of new land seemed irresistable to many. Economic conditions forced the migration of many settlers. While some of these people moved to other sections of Virginia, many removed to other states. The compiler has undertaken to present (with documentary proof) the names of as many of this latter group as can now be found in the records of southside Virginia.

When marriage records, wills, records of suits and some other documents are found, the compiler has included these documents with the hope that they may be of some value to those searching for Virginia ancestry. The compiler has not undertaken extensive research on any particular family. The records have been presented as a clue or basis for additional or continued research on such family lineage.

The migration from Virginia to other states falls primarily into five periods - pre-Revolutionary, post-Revolutionary, the period 1805-1830, pre-Civil War and post-Civil War. This latter period presents no particular problem to those interested in family research for nearly all of the county records are intact and the census records, 1850-1880, are readily available. Wars, fires and the ravages of time have taken a heavy toll of the earlier records which (with the loss of many of the parish records) makes it difficult now to find proof for many family names.

Virginia county clerks receive each year hundreds of requests for information on families. With an ever increasing work load (and many times with a limited staff), many of these requests necessarily remain unanswered even though the clerk may be sympathetic to such requests. He just does not have time to search records and answer many of these requests. Every assistance will be given and the county records are open to those who can take time to do their own research.

This volume was indexed and prepared for printing by my husband, Herbert A. Elliott.

Katherine B. Elliott

3

VIRGINIA COUNTY RECORDS

MECKLENBURG COUNTY

EARLY SETTLERS - Mecklenburg County, Vol. I	1964
EARLY SETTLERS - Mecklenburg County, Vol. II	1965
EARLY WILLS - 1765-1799 - Mecklenburg County	1963
MARRIAGE RECORDS, 1765-1810 - Mecklenburg County	1963
MARRIAGE RECORDS, 1811-1853 - Mecklenburg County	1962
REVOLUTIONARY WAR RECORDS - Mecklenburg County	1964

SOUTHSIDE VIRGINIA COUNTIES

EMIGRATION to OTHER STATES from SOUTHSIDE VIRGINIA

Volume I	1966
Volume II	1966
Volume III	

FUTURE VOLUMES

EARLY WILLS - Lunenburg County

Volume I

Volume II

Published and Sold by

Mrs. Katherine B. Elliott
P. O. Box 353
South Hill, Va. 23970

EMIGRANTS TO OTHER STATES

Volume II

Know all men by these presents that I, William
Alexander of the County of Putnam, State of Georgia, have
made, ordained, authorized, nominated and appointed Luke
Pryor of the County of Brunswick, State of Virginia, my true
and lawful attorney, for me and in my name, to ask, demand,
sue for, recover and receive of the administratrix of
Benjamin Lane, deceased, late of Brunswick County, State of
Virginia, all sums of money which are now due and owing to
me, the said William Alexander, from the said administratrix as fully and in every respect as if I were present in
person.
Dated 2 March 1810   Recorded 29 May 1810

Ref: Brunswick County Deed Book 21, page 52

Letters of administration is granted Silvia Lane on the
estate of Benjamin Lane, deceased.
Court 23 Oct. 1797

Ordered that William Meredith, Hartwell Bass, Burwell
Wilkes and Henry Hayes, or any three of them, being first
sworn, do appraise in current money the estate of Benjamin
Lane, deceased, and make report thereof to this Court.
Court 23 Oct. 1797

Ref: Brunswick County Order Book 17, page 397

M.B. 9 Dec. 1795 - Edmund Shell and Patsy Lane, daughter of
                   Benjamin Lane
            Surety: James Haldane
       Married 16 Dec. 1795 by the Rev. Aaron Brown

M.B. 14 Dec. 1799 - Edwin Fort and Lucy Lane
            Surety: Edmund Lane
       Married by the Rev. Ira Ellis

M.B. 18 Jan. 1802 - Sterling Harris and Sylvia Lane, widow
            Surety: Edmund Lane
       Married 22 Jan. 1802 by the Rev. Hubbard Saunders

M.B. 9 Nov. 1802 - William Alexander and Elizabeth Lane,
                   daughter of Sylvia Harris
            Surety: Edmund Lane
       Married 10 Nov. 1802 by the Rev. Aaron Brown

M.B. 2 Aug. 1808 - Luke Pryor and Nancy Lane
            Surety: Edmund Shell

Ref: Brunswick County Marriage Records, pages 89, 116,
     132, 136 and 167

ALLEN, James   Limestone County, Ala.

Know all men by these presents that I, James Allen of
the County of Limestone, State of Alabama, have made, constituted and appointed William Holt of Limestone County,
State of Alabama, my true and lawful attorney, for me and in
my name and stead, to ask, demand and receive all sums of
money due me in Greensville County, State of Virginia, and
to convey to Thomas Hill of Greensville County, State of
Virginia, all right and title in and to a tract of land in
Greensville County, and I hereby confirm whatsoever the
said Holt as my lawful attorney may do.
Dated 4 Feb. 1822   Recorded 7 Oct. 1822

Ref: Greensville County Deed Book 5, page 401

BARKSDALE, William   Warren County, Ga.

Be it known that I, William McKinney, of Charlotte
County, State of Virginia, hath constituted and appointed
William Barksdale of the County of Warren, State of Georgia,
my true and lawful attorney to sell a certain tract of land
lying and being in the County of Hancock, State of Georgia,
on the waters of Shoulderbone Creek containing $287\frac{1}{2}$ acres.
6 April 1801   Recorded 6 April 1801

Ref: Charlotte County Deed Book 9, page 17

William Barksdale of the Province of South Carolina to
John Barksdale of the County of Charlotte, State of Virginia
... cons. 75 pounds ... 145 acres more or less ... in the
Parish of Cornwall and County of Charlotte ... adjoining
Calvin Ford and Joseph Barksdale.
Dated 26 August 1779   Recorded 5 June 1780

Ref: Charlotte County Deed Book 4, page 217

William Barksdale of the Province of South Carolina to
Joseph Barksdale of Charlotte County, State of Virginia ...
cons. 75 pounds ... 145 acres more or less in Cornwall
Parish, County of Charlotte, State of Virginia ... adjoining
John Barksdale, et als.
Dated 26 August 1779   Recorded 5 June 1780

Ref: Charlotte County Deed Book 4, page 227

WILL OF COLLIER BARKSDALE

NAMES: Wife - Sarah Barksdale
       Sons - John Barksdale, William Barksdale and Nathan
              Barksdale
       Daughter - Lucy Barksdale - Daughter Allen

10

Plantation to wife Sarah Barksdale for life and after her
death to son John Barksdale.
Bequest - To son William Barksdale 300 acres of land.
        Specific bequests to other names.
Executors: Son William Barksdale and brothers John Barksdale
        and Hickson Barksdale
Witnesses: John Holt and Thomas Barksdale
Dated 1 July 1766   Recorded 3 Oct. 1774

    Ref: Charlotte County Will Book 1, page 117

BEDFORD, Robert   Bedford County, Tenn.

        Know all men by these presents that I, Robert Bedford
of the County of Bedford, State of Tennessee, for divers
good causes and considerations, have made, ordained, constituted and appointed my trusty friend and brother Clement
Read Bedford of the County of Rutherford, State of Tennessee
my true and lawful attorney in fact, for me and in my name
and for my use, to transact the following business:
        Whereas Thomas Read, late of Charlotte County, State of
Virginia, died intestate siezed and possessed of much goods
and chattels, land and tenements, I Robert Bedford being an
heir at law of the said estate, and
        Whereas Isaac Read and Clement Carrington, both of the
County of Charlotte, State of Virginia, were appointed administrators of the said Thomas Read, now I authorize and
empower the said Clement Read Bedford, my attorney, to ask,
demand and receive of the said administrators my distributive share of the said estate in my name and for my use.
Dated 9 July 1817   Recorded 3 Aug. 1819

    Ref: Charlotte County Deed Book 15, page 166

M.B. 6 February 1783 - Robert Bedford and Mary Hill Read,
                        daughter of M. Read *
                        Surety: James Hamlett
        Married 27 Feb. 1783 by the Rev. Thomas Johnston
        Robert Bedford, son of Stephen Bedford, deceased.

* Mary (Nash) Read widow of Clement Read, Junr.

Note: Mary Hill Read (named for her grandmother) was the
        daughter of Clement Read, Junr., and Mary Nash, (dau-
        ghter of John Nash of Prince Edward County), and the
        granddaughter of Clement Read, Senr., and Mary Hill.

                WILL OF STEPHEN BEDFORD

NAMES: Wife - Frances Bedford
        Son - Robert Bedford
        Daughters - Rebecca Bedford, Sally Bedford, Frances

                        11

Bedford
Mentions unborn child *
Executors: Wife Frances Bedford, brother Thomas Bedford,
       friends Sherwood Walton and Joseph Pearson
Witnesses: Robert Walton, Sherwood Walton, John Sullivant
Dated 4 June 1772   Recorded 3 May 1773

        Ref: Charlotte County Will Book 1, page 101

* Clement Read Bedford

5 May 1756 - Stephen Bedford, Junr. and Frances Walker
           Peterson

22 December 1757 - Clement Read, Junr. and Mary Nash

        Ref: Lunenburg County Marriage Records, 1746-1761

M.B. 20 June 1774 - Diggs Bumpass and Frances Bedford, widow
                  of Stephen Bedford
                  Surety: John Williams

M.B. 13 December 1780 - Thomas Ligon and Fanny Bumpass
                      Surety: James Hamlett

        Ref: Charlotte County Marriage Records, pages 24-38

Note: "THE READS and their RELATIVES" (an account of the an-
      cestry and descendants of Clement Read, Senr.) states
      (footnote page 271) that Frances Bedford, widow of
      Stephen Bedford, married (2) Thomas Ligon, Junr., but
      this is in error as she married (2) Diggs Bumpass and
      (3) Thomas Ligon.

RUCKER, James   Rutherford County, Tenn.

     Know all men by these presents that we, James Rucker
and Lucy L. Rucker, formerly Lucy L. Bedford, of Rutherford
County, State of Tennessee, do by these presents ordain,
constitute and appoint Clement R. Bedford of Rutherford
County, State of Tennessee, our true and lawful attorney for
and in our names but to our use to ask, demand, sue for, re-
recover and receive of the administrators of the estate of
Col. Thomas Read, deceased, late of Charlotte County, State
of Virginia, all of any part of Lucy LeGrand Bedford's distributive share of the said estate, and to give discharges
for the same as fully as if we were present in person, and
we ratify and confirm whatsoever our attorney may lawfully
do in the premises.
Dated 14 July 1817   Recorded 3 Aug. 1819

        Ref: Charlotte County Deed Book 15, page 166

ADDAMAN, Thomas   Granville County, N. C.

Thomas Addaman and Hannah Addaman, his wife, of Granville County, Province of North Carolina, to Henry Wilson of
Lunenburg County, Colony of Virginia ... cons. 15 pounds ...
174 acres ... adjoining William Rose on the county (Granville) line.
Dated 6 December 1757   Recorded 6 Dec. 1757

    Ref: Lunenburg County Deed Book 5, page 97

Thomas, son of Thomas and Mary Adaman, born 6 October 1724.

    Ref: Bristol Parish Register, page 275

Thomas Addaman, Senr., died before 5 February 1735 when
an inventory of his estate was returned to the Brunswick
County Court by Mary Addaman, administratrix.

    Ref: Brunswick County, Wills, Deeds, etc., Book 1,
         page 250

There are no known extant marriage records for Thomas
Addaman, Senr., to Mary, or of Thomas Addaman, Junr., to
Hannah, and their names are unknown. Mary Addaman, widow
of Thomas Addaman, married (2) Thomas Stephens.

List of tithes taken in 1748 by Lewis Delony for that
part of Cumberland Parish, Lunenburg (now Mecklenburg) County lists
              Thomas Stephens   )
)   2 tithes
              Thomas Addiman   )

Thomas Stephens died before 3 August 1758, and an inventory of his estate was returned to the Court of Lunenburg
County 2 June 1761.

Theophilus Feild of Prince George County to Mary
Stevens (Stephens), widow, of Lunenburg County ... cons. 67
pounds 9 shillings 9 pence ... 1004 acres of land granted to
Theophilus Feild by patent 26 June 1755.
Witnesses: Theop⁵ Feild, Junr., Thomas Addaman, John Cunn-
           ingham
Dated 3 August 1758   Recorded 5 Dec. 1758

    Ref: Lunenburg County Deed Book 5, page 348

FEILD, Theophilus - 26 June 1755 - 1004 acres on the south
                    side of the Roanoke River on Nutbush
                    Creek.

    Ref: Patent Book 31, page 443 - Va. State Library

13

WILL OF MARY STEVENS (STEPHENS)

NAMES: Son - Thomas Addaman
        Daughter - Mourning Matthews
        Grandson - William Kidd
        Bequests made to Thomas Addaman, Mourning Matthews
        and William Kidd
        Sons - John Stevens, Thomas Stevens (Stephens)
        Land and remainder of estate to two sons John and
        Thomas Stevens.
Executors: Sons John Stephens and Thomas Stephens
Witnesses: John Johnson, Thomas Carter, Elizabeth Johnson
Dated 4 August 1791   Recorded 10 Oct. 1791

        Ref: Mecklenburg County Will Book 2, page 76

Note: Thomas Addaman living in Stokes County, N. C., in 1790

        Ref: Stokes County, N. C., Census 1790

        Deborah Stevens granted administration on the estate of
Thomas Stevens, deceased, and with William Hendrick, her
security, gave bond in amount of 500 pounds.
                                        Court 12 Jan. 1795

        Ref: Mecklenburg County Fiduciary Book - unpaged

Wards		Guardian	Bond
STEPHENS,	Joshua	William Hendrick	9-14-1795
"	, Deborah	"	9-14-1795
"	, Joseph	"	9-14-1795
"	, Haley	"	9-14-1795

        Ref: Mecklenburg County Guardian Book - unpaged

CHANCERY SUIT

        John Stephens, John Carter and Polly Carter, his wife,
Plaintiffs,
                                VS
        Joshua Stephens, Debby Stephens, Joseph Stephens and
Hailey Stephens, Infants under the age of 21 years by Debby
Stephens, their guardian, and the said Debby Stephens, widow
of Thomas Stephens, deceased, Defendants.

        In conforming to the Court Order of August 1797, we the
Commissioners sold (after advertising) the 200 acres of land
at Public Auction to John Johnson for the sum of 2,075
pounds, 14 Dec. 1797.   /s/ William Davis
Costs to be borne jointly   John Davis, Junr.
by both parties.   Christopher Haskins
                                        Court 12 May 1799

        Ref: Mecklenburg County Order Book 10, page 142

14

M.B. 12 December 1788 - John Carter and Polly Stevens
                        Surety: Thomas Stevens

    Ref: ELLIOTT: Mecklenburg County Marriage Records,
                  1765-1810, page 27

M.B. 13 January 1801 - Joshua Stevens and Fanny Kitchen
                        Surety: Thomas Carter

    Ref: Granville County, N. C., Marriage Records

Note: Deborah Stevens, widow of Thomas Stevens, with her
      sons Joseph and Hailey Stevens and daughter Deborah
      Stevens removed to Georgia before 1806.

BALL, Isaac   Wilkes County, Ga.

    Know all men by these presents that I, Isaac Ball of
the County of Wilkes, State of Georgia, administrator of the
estate of James Armstrong, deceased, late of the State of
South Carolina, have made, nominated and appointed my friend
William Peters Martin of Halifax County, State of Virginia,
my true and lawful attorney, for me as administrator aforesaid, to receive all moneys, etc., due to the estate of
James Armstrong, deceased.
Dated 29 March 1784   Recorded 21 Oct. 1784

    Ref: Halifax County Deed Book 13, page 89

BASKERVILL, Robert E.   Edgefield District, S. C.

City of Augusta,
State of Georgia:
                Know all men by these presents that I,
Robert E. Baskervill of Edgefield District, State of South
Carolina, for divers good causes and considerations, me
thereunto moving, have appointed Samuel H. Warren of Mecklenburg County, State of Virginia, my lawful attorney to
collect from any person who has it in his possession that
portion of the estate of Betsy Baskervill, late of Mecklenburg County, deceased, to which I am entitled consisting of
land, slaves and other property.
Dated 7 September 1842   Recorded 20 Feb. 1843

Power of Attorney witnessed by

     Benjamin B. Russell, Dept. Clerk, Richmond County, Ga.
     Benjamin H. Warren, One of the Presiding Justices,
                                      Richmond County, Ga.

    Ref: Mecklenburg County Deed Book 30, page 177

BEASLEY, Nancy   Madison County, Ky.

    Know all men by these presents that I, Nancy Beasley,
of the County of Madison, Commonwealth of Kentucky, for
divers good causes and considerations, have made, ordained,
constituted and appointed my trusty friend Richard Hart of
Madison County, Commonwealth of Kentucky, my true and lawful
attorney, for me and in my name and to my use, to ask, dem-
and and receive of and from every person in the State of
Virginia who has charge, all land that may descend to me as
heir of John Beasley, deceased, or given to me by the will
of the said John Beasley. And I give my attorney full power and authority to collect all sums coming to me as heir of
my father William Beasley, deceased, and I ratify and confirm whatsoever my attorney shall lawfully do.
Dated 4 October 1813   Recorded 9 March 1814

   Ref: <u>Charlotte County Deed Book 13, page 36</u>

WILL OF JOHN BEASLEY

NAMES: Wife - not named in will and evidently deceased
       Daughter Elizabeth wife of Alexander Clayton
       Sons - Charles Beasley, Gabriel Beasley, Cornelius
          Beasley
       Daughter - Sarah Fowlkes
       Son - William Beasley, deceased
       Grandchildren - John Beasley, Thomas Beasley, Polly
       Beasley, Nancy Beasley, Betsy Beasley, children of
       my son William Beasley.
       Grandchildren - John Clayton, Sally Clayton, child-
       ren of my daughter Elizabeth.
Executors: Joseph Reynolds and Stephen Farmer
Witnesses: William Hart, Beasley Hart, Thomas Hart, Reuben
       Hart
Dated 24 February 1801   Recorded 3 March 1801

   Ref: <u>Charlotte County Will Book 2, page 193</u>

M.B. 6 January 1806 - Joseph Cheatham and Elizabeth Beasley,
               widow
               Surety: Richard Hart
     Married 9 January 1806 by the Rev. Richard Dabbs, Jr.

   Ref: <u>Charlotte County Marriage Records, page 396</u>

Note: While the record does not so state, Elizabeth Beasley,
   who married Joseph Cheatham was probably the widow of
   William Beasley named in the will of John Beasley.
     Nancy Beasley, who gave power of attorney, was prob-
   ably her daughter, but not researched.

BONNER, Jeremiah   Baldwin County, Ga.

     Jeremiah Bonner of the State of Georgia and County of
Baldwin, and Sarah Bonner, his wife, to Robert Hale of the
County of Sussex, State of Virginia ... cons. 200 pounds ...
100 acres lying and being in Sussex County, State of Vir-
ginia ... adjoining Tyus, Hill, William Echols, Joel Echols,
et als.
Witnesses: Jesse Wren(n)   /s/ Jeremiah Bonner
           Jonathon Harris   Sarah (X) Bonner
           Nathan Wren(n)
Dated 24 Februsry 1808   Recorded 5 May 1808

     Ref: Sussex County Deed Book "K", page 164

M.B. 4 August 1772 - Jeremiah Bonner and Sally Hall, dau. of
                     James Hall
                     Surety: James Hall

     Ref: Sussex County Marriage Records, page 15

M.B. 19 January 1774 - James Hall and Elizabeth Owen, widow

M.B. 20 April 1773 - James Bonner and Mary Jones, dau. of
                     James Jones
                     Surety: Jeremiah Bonner

M.B. 9 February 1756 - John Bonner and Mary Briggs, widow
                       Surety: William Bonner

     Ref: Sussex County Marriage Records, pages 1, 17, 18

     John Brown of Lunenburg County to Jeremiah Bonner of
Charlotte County ... cons. 15,000 pounds of Inspected Tobacco ... a tract of 150 acres of land on Nelsons Creek, and
on the north side of the Middle Meherrin River.
Dated 15 December 1784   Recorded 12 May 1785

     Ref: Lunenburg County Deed Book 14, page 211

     Jeremiah Bonner of Charlotte County to Robert Wilson,
Senr., of Lunenburg County ... cons. 18,000 pounds of net
Inspected Tobacco ... 150 acres of land on Nelsons Creek
and on north side of Middle Meherrin.
Witness: James Bonner
Dated 6 March 1788   Recorded 12 June 1788

     Ref: Lunenburg County Deed Book 15, page 222

     Sally Bonner, wife of Jeremiah Bonner, released her
dower right in this land.   Recorded 9 Sept. 1788

     Ref: Lunenburg County Deed Book 15, page 511

17

Know all men by these presents that I, Wilson Bottom of Henderson County, State of Kentucky, have appointed John Winckler of Mecklenburg County, State of Virginia, my lawful attorney to ask, demand, recover and receive of Christopher Haskins of Mecklenburg County State of Virginia, administrator of the estate of Wilkerson Bottom (my father) all or any part of the legacy due me, and further, at the death of my mother Mary Bottom, the said John Winckler shall act for my interest in her estate, and also her dower from the estate of Wilkerson Bottom, deceased, which may be in her hands at the time of her death.

Dated 10 April 1821   Recorded 1 May 1821

Ref: Mecklenburg County Deed Book 19, page 82

Mary Bottom, widow and relict of Wilkerson Bottom, deceased, Plaintiff

VS

Christopher Haskins administrator of Wilkerson Bottom, deceased, Anderson Bottom, Wilson Bottom, Anselm Roberts and Nancy Bottom, his wife, Defendants.

Commissioners were appointed to lay off and allot to Mary Bottom her dower in estate of Wilkerson Bottom.

Ref: Mecklenburg County Order Book 20, page 348

Wilson Bottom and Elizabeth Bottom, his wife, of Henderson County, State of Kentucky, to Patrick H. Foster of Mecklenburg County, State of Virginia, cons. $275.00 ... 55 acres and 120 poles ... being Lot No 3 recently purchased of Anderson Bottom, one of the legatees of Wilkerson Bottom, deceased.

Dated 8 October 1821   Recorded 8 Oct. 1821

Ref: Mecklenburg County Deed Book 19, page 244

M.B. 22 July 1806 - Anselm Roberts and Nancy Bottom
                    Surety: Hughberry Nanney
          Married 23 July 1806 by the Rev. James Meacham

M.B. 20 Dec. 1806 - Wilson Bottom and Elizabeth Richardson
                    Surety: Nathaniel Moss

M.B. 30 May 1809 - Anderson Bottom and Sally Hatchell
                    Surety: William H. Bugg
          Married 31 May 1809 by the Rev. James Meacham

Ref: ELLIOTT, Mecklenburg County Marriage Records,
          1765-1810, pages 17 and 105

BAIN, Elijah   Belmont County, Ohio

Know all men by these presents that I, Elijah Bain of
Belmont County, State of Ohio, and guardian of Eldridge
Wootton and Miranda Wootton, minors, and heirs of Edward
Wootton, deceased, late of Sussex County, State of Virginia,
and
Whereas Eldridge and Miranda Wootton, heirs of the said
Edward Wootton, are entitled by law to an undivided two-
thirds of the land of Edward Wootton, deceased,
Know ye that I, Elijah Bain the guardian of the said
Eldridge and Miranda, do appoint my brother Samuel Bain of
the County of Sussex, State of Virginia, my lawful attorney,
in my name as the guardian of Eldridge and Miranda Wootton,
to sell and convey all title to the said tract of land in
Sussex County and to collect all money due to the said orphans above named.

Dated 30 September 1815   /s/ Elijah Bain, guardian of
Witnesses: Eldridge and Miranda Woot-
   Nicholas Presson   ton, acting under authority
   James White   from the Court of Belmont
   William Dobie   County, State of Ohio
                                    Recorded 7 March 1816

   Ref: Sussex County Deed Book "M", page 40

               WILL OF EDWARD WOOTTON

NAMES: Wife - mentioned in will but not by name.
       Sons - George Wootton, Eldridge Wootton
       Daughter - Miranda Wootton
       Bequests to the three children - Balance of estate to
       wife for her natural life.
Executors: Wife (not named) and John Bain
Witnesses: Elijah Bain and John Watkins
Dated 15 April 1804   Recorded 4 Oct. 1804

   Ref: Sussex County Will Book "F", page 427

WOOTTON, George   Belmont County, Ohio

Know all men by these presents whereas I, George Wootton of Belmont County, State of Ohio, am siezed in fee of a
third part of a certain tract or parcel of land situate in
Sussex County, State of Virginia, formerly in the possession
of Edward Wootton, deceased, now
Know ye that I George Wootton, one of the legal heirs
of the said Edward Wootton, deceased, have by these presents
made, constituted and appointed Elijah Bain my true and lawful attorney, for me and in my name and for my use, to sell
and dispose of the said tract of land.
Dated 18 August 1815   Recorded 7 March 1816

M.B. 19 Dec. 1781 - John Bain and Sylvia Wooten, daughter of
                    Edward Wooten *
                    Surety: Nicholas Presson

M.B. 29 Oct. 1789 - Edward Wootton, Jr. and Abigail Bailey
                    Surety: John Bain
                    Consent: Milley Sears

M.B. 18 March 1807 - Elijah Bain and Rhoda Brock
                     Surety: Lemuel Bain
                     Consent: James Brock

M.B. 4 April 1805 - James White, Jr. and Levina Bain
                    Surety: Elijah Bain
       Married 11 April by the Rec. Jesse Halleman, Senr.

* This was probably Edward Wootton, Senr., and the Edward of
  the foregoing will was Edward Wootton, Junr. Research in
  the records of Sussex and Surry Counties would have to be
  made, however, to determine family relationship. The name
  Wootton is recorded variously as Wooten, Wootton and as
  Wooton.

<u>BROWN, Henry</u>   <u>Davidson County, Tenn.</u>

     Know all men by these presents that I, Henry Brown of
Davidson County, State of Tennessee, have made, constituted
and appointed my trusty friend and brother James Brown, for
me and in my name, to ask, demand and receive all sums of
money, debts and goods, wheresoever they may be found, coming to me as one of the heirs of my late father William
Brown, late of Isle of Wight County, State of Virginia.
Dated 31 May 1815   Recorded 2 Oct. 1815

<u>BROWN, James</u> et als   <u>Williamson County, Tenn.</u>

     Know all men by these presents that we, Henry Brown,
James Brown and Henry Moss of the County of Williamson,
State of Tennessee, do appoint our brother William Brown of
Sussex County, State of Virginia, our true and lawful attor-
ney to collect all money coming to us as legatees of our
uncle, John Holt, deceased, whose estate is in the County of
Sussex, and to take any legal steps necessary.
Dated 7 March 1829   Recorded 2 April 1829

     Ref: <u>Sussex County Deed Book "P", page 384</u>

M.B. 25 August 1796 - Henry Brown and Patty Eggleston
            Surety: William Brown

M.B. 4 January 1809 - Henry Moss and Abba Browne, daughter
            of William Browne
            Surety: Hinchey Knight

Ref: Sussex County Marriage Records, pp. 83--131

FOWLKES, Gabriel et als   Giles County, Tenn.

    Gabriel Fowlkes, Thompson Fowlkes, John G. Fowlkes,
Joseph Fowlkes and George Malone and Sarah Malone, his wife,
which said Gabriel Fowlkes, Thompson Fowlkes, John G. Fowlkes, Joseph Fowlkes and Sarah Malone are heirs and representatives of Thompson Fowlkes, deceased, sell to Nathan
Fowlkes ... cons. $1,000.00 ... 492 acres on the waters of
Otter Creek ... adjoining James Garner, Senr., Thomas Brough
Dr. Hugh Nelson, Richard Russell and Thomas Toone ... being
the tract of land on which the said Thompson Fowlkes, Senr.,
deceased, lived.
Witnesses: /s/ Gabriel Fowlkes
    Elisha White   Thompson Fowlkes
    John C. Walker   John G. Fowlkes
    Hume R. Field   Joseph Fowlkes
                                      George Malone
                                      Sarah Malone

Dated 26 May 1817

    Giles County Court 1 Dec. 1817
                                    John C. Walker and
Elisha White, two of the witnesses, appeared in open Court
and made oath that they heard the grantees therein named
acknowledge their signatures.
                        /s/ German Lester Clk

    Sarah Malone, wife of George Malone, was examined by
Joseph Rear and John Hillhouse, Justices of the Peace for
Giles County, since she could not conveniently travel to the
Mecklenburg County Court, and she freely relinguished her
dower right 26 May 1817.

    This indenture proved by the oath of Hume R. Feild, a
witness, and together with certificates of proof from the
Court of Giles County, State of Tennessee, ordered to be
recorded.
                        /s/ Joel Watkins Clk
                            Recorded 19 Jan. 1818

    Ref: Mecklenburg County Deed Book 17, page 163

BUTLER, Winifred   Edgefield District, S. C.

        Know all men by these presents that I, Winifred Butler
of Edgefield District, State of South Carolina, do appoint
David Thomas of Brunswick County, State of Virginia, my true
and lawful attorney to sue for, and execute a bill of sale
of, a negro which fell to my share under the last will and
testament of my deceased father, Robert Brooks, late of
Brunswick County, State of Virginia, and due me at the death
of my stepmother, Abigail Brooks.
Dated 6 April 1819   Recorded May Court 1819

        Ref: Brunswick County Deed Book 24, page 307

                    WILL OF ROBERT BROOKS

NAMES; Wife - Abigail Brooks
        Sons - Wade Brooks, William Brooks
        Daughters - Sarah White, Mary White, Lucy Baugh,
        Winifred Butler, Rebekah Thomas, Penelope Jones
        Jincy (Jane) Lambert
Land - 550 acres on Roanoke River and 283 acres which I
        bought of John Eppes to be sold.
Home plantation and land I bought of Hicks Ellis left to
wife Abigail Brooks for her natural life and then to my
grandson Robert Brooks, son of Wade Brooks.
        Slaves and personal property left to wife, and
after her death to be divided among all children.
        Money arising from sale of land, slaves and person-
al property (not given to wife) to be divided as follows:
        1. To daughter Lucy Baugh $2.00.
        2. To the children of my daughter Sarah White one-
           eighth part.
        3. To my daughter Mary White one-eighth part.
        4. To my daughter Winifred Butler one-eighth part.
        5. To my son William Brooks one-eighth part.
        6. To my daughter Rebekah Thomas one-eighth part.
        7. To my daughter Penelope Jones one-eighth part.
        8. To my son Wade Brooks one-eighth part.
        9. To my daughter Jincy Lambert one-eighth part.
Executors: Son-in-law David Thomas and Ebenezer McGowan
Dated 11 May 1804   Recorded 9 June 1806

        Ref: Mecklenburg County Will Book 5, page 354

Note: Ebenezer McGowan qualified as executor on the estate
      of Robert Brooks, deceased, 14 July 1806, with William
      Davis and Richard Fox his securities, giving bond in
      the penalty of $20,000.00.
        Ebenezer McGowan moved later to Tennessee, and
David Thomas qualified as executor on the unsettled estate
19 Jan. 1829 with David W. Thomas and Sterling Crowder his
securities giving bond in the penalty of $5,000.00.

Michael Young of Isle of Wight County to Robert Brooks of Mecklenburg County ... cons. 100 pounds ... 100 acres on a branch of Poplar Creek in Brunswick County ... adjoining Thomas Harrison, James Harwell, Grief Harwell and others.
Witnesses: James Young
            Charles Portlock   /s/ Michael Young
            Robert Cheek
Dated 23 Nov. 1778   Recorded 23 Nov. 1778

Ref: Brunswick County Deed Book 13, page 217

Robert Brooks and Brambly Brooks, his wife, of Mecklenburg County to Thomas Harrison of Brunswick County ... cons. 100 pounds ... 100 acres on the lower side of Little Creek (a branch of Poplar Creek) ... adjoining James Harwell, Travis Love and Grief Harwell.
Witnesses: James Harwell   /s/ Robert Brooks
            Grief Harwell   Brambly Brooks
Dated 18 May 1779   Recorded 22 Nov. 1779

Ref: Brunswick County Deed Book 13, page 408

ELLIS, Hix (Hicks)   Warren County, N. C.

Hicks Ellis and Nancy Ellis, his wife, of Warren County, State of North Carolina, to Robert Brooks of Mecklenburg County, State of Virginia, ... cons. 8000 cwt of inspected Tobacco ... 175 acres, more or less, at the mouth of the long branch ... on the line of Robert Brooks, and adjoining Harwell and Lambert ... graveyard reserved.
Witnesses: John Webb   /s/ Hicks Ellis
            David Thomas
Dated 28 February 1786   Recorded 10 April 1786

Ref: Mecklenburg County Deed Book 7, page 32

Tithe list taken by Edmund Taylor for year 1764 in St. James Parish, Lunenburg (now Mecklenburg) County.

     James Ellis   )
           John Robinson) 2 tithes - 170 acres of land

Ref: ELLIOTT: Early Settlers, Mecklenburg County,
            Volume I, page 154

Administration granted Abigail Ellis on the estate of James Ellis, deceased.
                      Court 12 Oct. 1778

Ref: Mecklenburg County Order Book 4, page 441

Ordered that James Baugh, Daniel Baugh, John Smith and Frederick Rainey, or any three of them, being first sworn, do appraise in current Money the slaves and personal estate of James Ellis, deceased, and return report to Court.

Court 12 Oct. 1778

Ref: <u>Mecklenburg County Order Book 4, page 441</u>

Inventory and appraisal of the estate of James Ellis, deceased, returned to Court and ordered to be recorded.

Court 8 March 1779

Ref: <u>Mecklenburg County Will Book 1, page 293</u>

Mecklenburg County Census taken by Lewis Parham in Oct. 1782.

Robert Brooks	Head of family 7 persons	17 slaves
Abigail Ellis	do	10 do	0 do

Ref: ELLIOTT: Early Settlers, Mecklenburg County,
Volume II, pages 206-207

Mecklenburg County Personal Property Tax Lists:

Year 1783	- Abigail Ellis	Listed
1784	- Abigail Ellis	Not Listed

Note: All of the records of St. James Parish, Mecklenburg County, have been lost, and there are no vital records now extant. Brambly Brooks, wife of Robert Brooks, died by 1783, and Robert Brooks married (2) Abigail Ellis, widow of James Ellis. There is no extant record of the marriage of Robert Brooks to Abigail Ellis.

Robert Brooks and Abigail Brooks, his wife, of Mecklenburg County, to Joseph Lambert of Mecklenburg County ....
cons. 40 pounds ... 100 acres ... on the long branch.
Witnesses: John Smith   /s/
           Charles Coppage   /s/
<u>Dated 5 March 1790</u>   Recorded 12 April 1790

Ref: <u>Mecklenburg County Deed Book 12, page 571</u>

<u>CHANCERY SUIT</u>

Abigail Brooks, widow and relict of Robert Brooks, deceased, Plaintiff

VS

Ebenezer McGowan, executor, Winny Brooks who married James Butler, Polly Brooks who married Burgess White, Rebecca Brooks who married David Thomas, Nelly Brooks who married Frederick Jones, Jane Brooks who married Julius Lambert, the children of B(lumer) White who married another daughter now deceased, the children of Wade Brooks, son of Robert Brooks, and the children

24

of William Brooks another son, Defendants.

Suit for the allotment of the widow's dower.

Court 9 Oct. 1809

Ref: Mecklenburg County Deed Book 15, page 69

BROOKS, Robert   Edgefield District, S. C.

Know all men by these presents that I, Robert Brooks of
Edgefield District, State of South Carolina, have appointed
David Thomas of Brunswick County, State of Virginia, my lawful attorney to sue for, collect and receive from Ebenezer
McGowan, executor of the estate of Robert Brooks, Senr.,
deceased, late of Mecklenburg County, State of Virginia, my
respective share, and as attorney for my brothers and sisters, or one-eighth part of the estate of the decedant as the
respective share or legal amount of our father William
Brooks, deceased, and David Thomas is to carry out all legal
acts as if he were doing it.
Dated 12 January 1809   Recorded 13 March 1809

Ref: Mecklenburg County Deed Book 14, page 33

CHANCERY SUIT

David Thomas and wife Rebecca, James Butler and wife
Winifred, Burgess White and wife Mary, Frederick Jones and
wife Penelope and Julius Lambert and wife Jane, Plaintiffs
Vs
Ebenezer McGowan, executor of the estate of Robert
Brooks, deceased, the representative of Wade Brooks and
William Brooks, which two were sons and legatees of Robert
Brooks, deceased, and the heirs of Sarah White, deceased.

Suit for the division of the slaves in the estate of
Robert Brooks, deceased.

Court 1 Jan. 1807

Division made by James Harwell, Grief Harwell, John
Aldridge and Richard Baugh, Commissioners, appointed by the
Court.

M.B. 10 October 1780 - Daniel Baugh and Lucy Brooks
                       Surety: John Eppes

M.B. 16 October 1787 - Frederick Jones and Nelly Brooks
                       Surety: Jourdain Brooks

M.B. 13 December 1796 - Julius Lambert and Jincy Brooks
                       Surety: John McKinney

Ref: ELLIOTT: Mecklenburg County Marriage Records,
        1765-1810, pages 14, 74, 79

CARDWELL, George   State of Ky.

    Know all men by these presents that I, George Cardwell
of the State of Kentucky for divers good causes, me hereunto
moving, have nominated, constituted and appointed Josiah
LeGrand of Charlotte County, State of Virginia, my true and
lawful attorney, for me and in my name and for my use, and
as executor of Richard Cardwell, deceased, to collect all
sums due to the estate of Richard Cardwell, deceased, and to
receive all property that shall remain in the said estate at
the death of my mother Susannah Cardwell, and to distribute
the money arising in the said estate agreeable to the will
of the said Richard Cardwell, deceased, and my attorney is
to perform all things as fully as if I were present and personally acting.
Dated 26 November 1805   Recorded 7 July 1806

        Ref: Charlotte County Deed Book 10, page 230

                    WILL OF RICHARD CARDWELL

NAMES: Wife - Susannah Cardwell
       Daughter - Penelope Clark
       Sons - Thomas Cardwell, Peter Cardwell
       Daughter Maryann Cardwell
       Sons - Daniel Cardwell, George Cardwell
Executors: Sons Daniel and George Cardwell and wife Susannah
           Cardwell
Witnesses: Obedience Cardwell, Martha Perrin Parker and
           William Parker
Dated (month & day not given) 1780   Recorded 3 April 1780

        Ref: Charlotte County Will Book 1, page 220

M.B. 17 March 1789 - Obediah Chisolm and Mary Ann Cardwell,
                     daughter of Richard and Susanna
                     Cardwell
                     Surety: Francis Jackson

    Ref: Charlotte County Marriage Records, page 133

Note: On August 19, 1729, Thomas Cardwell of Henrico County
    purchased of Warham Easley 400 acres of land on Deep
    Creek in Goochland (now Cumberland) County. On July 20,
    1745, by deed of gift, Thomas Cardwell gave each of his
    sons, viz: Richard Cardwell, Thomas Perrin Cardwell,
    John Cardwell and George Cardwell, 100 acres of land on
    Deep Creek.

    Thomas Cardwell of Henrico County ... for the natural
love and affection I have for my son Richard Cardwell ......
gives to Richard Cardwell 100 acres on branches of Deep

Creek in Goochland County ... which I purchased of Warham
Easley.
Dated 20 July 1745

Ref: Goochland County Deed Book 5, page 7

John LeGrand of Halifax County to Richard Cardwell of
Cumberland County ... cons. 12 pounds 10 shillings ... 300
acres in Halifax County ... on both sides of Beaverdam
Branch ... being part of the land granted to John LeGrand by
patent.
Dated 21 November 1752

Ref: Halifax County Deed Book 1, page 13

Note: Richard Cardwell of Cumberland County sold this land
in 1756.

CLEMENTS, William   Montgomery County, Tenn.

Know all men by these presents that I, William R. B.
Clements of Mecklenburg County, State of Virginia, have appointed David C. Hutcheson of Montgomery County, State of
Tennessee, my true and lawful attorney to receive all money
or property which descended to me, or was devised to me,
from the estate of William Clements, deceased, my late father, of Montgomery County, State of Tennessee, now in the
hands of Christopher Clements, John C. Collier and Robert
West, executors of the estate of William Clements, deceased.
Witnesses:
    R. Apperson   /s/ Wm R. B. Clements
    N^m Dortch
Dated 3 November 1823   Recorded 20 Nov. 1823

Ref: Mecklenburg County Deed Book 20, page 356

M.B. 5 June 1789 - William Clements and Sarah Bignal
              Surety: Joseph Speed
      Married 5 June 1789 by the Rev. Thomas Scott

Ref: ELLIOTT: Mecklenburg County Marriage Records,
              1765-1810, page 31

M.B. 5 Nov. 1814 - William R. B. Clements and Sally A. Green
              Surety: Henry Wilson
              Consent: Howell P. Harper guardian of
                       Sally A(nn) Green
      Married 7 Nov. 1814 by the Rev. Charles Ogburn

Ref: ELLIOTT: Mecklenburg County Marriage Records,
              1811-1853, page 36

CHAPPELL, James   Davidson County, Tenn.

Know all men by these presents that I, James Chappell
of the County of Davidson, State of Tennessee, do appoint
Clement McDaniel of Pittsylvania County, State of Virginia,
my attorney to ask, demand and receive of Thomas H. Wooding
of Pittsylvania County, executor of the last will and testament of Robert Wooding, deceased, late of Halifax County,
State of Virginia, all of the legacy devised by the said
Robert Wooding, deceased, in the last will and testament to
the children of James Chappell and Martha his wife. Clement
McDaniel is to represent me as though I was there in person.
Dated 6 March 1800   Recorded 21 April 1800
      Ref: Pittsylvania County Loose Papers - 1799-1801
                      Virginia State Library

M.B. 22 Jan. 1781 - James Chappell and Martha Wooding
                    Daughter of Robert Wooding
        Ref: Halifax County Marriage Records, page 5

DALEY, Josiah   Limestone County, Ala.

Know all men by these presents that I, Josiah Daley of
Limestone County, State of Alabama, do appoint David Moore,
of Mecklenburg County State of Virginia, my lawful attorney
to ask, demand and sue for my proportionate part of the
estate of Ambrose Daley, deceased, of whom I am one of the
legatees.
Dated 21 September 1824   Recorded 17 Jan. 1825
      Ref: Mecklenburg County Deed Book 21, page 209

MOORE, Feild   Wake County, N. C.

Know all men by these presents that I, Feild Moore of
the County of Wake, State of North Carolina, Planter, do
appoint Godfrey Crowder of Mecklenburg County, State of
Virginia, my lawful attorney to collect for me any money due
to me in the State of Virginia.
Dated 22 March 1792   Recorded 10 Sept. 1792
      Ref: Mecklenburg County Deed Book 8, page 201

Feild Moore and Sarah his wife of Mecklenburg County to
James Hall of Mecklenburg County ... cons. 275 pounds ....
102½ acres on Little Bluestone Creek.
Dated 14 December 1778   Recorded 13 April 1779
      Ref: Mecklenburg County Deed Book 5, page 415

M.B. 26 November 1774 - Feild Moore and Sarah Lidderdale
                    Surety: Thomas Moore
        Consent: Thomas Anderson guardian of Sarah
      Ref: ELLIOTT: Mecklenburg County Marriage Records,
                      1765-1810, page 89

WARD	GUARDIAN	DATE
Sarah Lidderdale	Thomas Anderson	6-10-1765

Orphan of William Lidderdale, deceased
Ref: ELLIOTT: Early Settlers, Vol. II, page 166

NOTE: Heads of Families - North Carolina

MOORE, Feild - Males over 16 (1) Under 16 (2) Females (3)
      Ref: Wake County, N. C. - Census 1790

WILL of THOMAS MOORE

NAMES: Wife - not named in will
        Children - Thomas Moore, Seth Moore, Taffanus Hudson,
              Elizabeth Davis, Prescilla Nunn
        Six younger children - George Moore, Feild Moore,
        Judith Boyd, Nancy Crowder, Mary Franklin, Lucy
        Willis
Executors: Godfrey Crowder, George Moore, Hugh Franklin
Dated 31 March 1793   Recorded 13 July 1795
      Ref: Mecklenburg County Will Book 3, page 272

HAILEY, Phillip R. et als   Rutherford County, Tenn.

      Phillip R. Hailey of Rutherford County, State of Tenn-
essee, attorney in fact for Susanna Foster, James Foster,
Anne Foster, Henry Wyatt and Susannah Wyatt, his wife, Peggy
Foster, John Foster in right of his wife Elizabeth Foster,
now deceased, acting under a Power of Attorney recorded in
Rutherford County, State of Tennessee, for and in consideration of $125.00, bargains, grants and sells to Robert
Hairston of Henry County, State of Virginia, a certain tract
of land on Leatherwood Creek in Henry County containing 138
acres ... as evidenced by two deeds - (1) for 86 acres and
(2) for 52 acres - being the land conveyed by Thomas Wilkins
to Thomas Foster, now deceased.
Dated 20 December 1824   Recorded 20 Dec. 1824

      Ref: Henry County Deed Book 10, page 83

      Thomas Foster died intestate in 1812. Inventory and ap-
praisal of the estate of Thomas Foster, deceased, which was
ordered at the March Court 1812 for Henry County, returned
to Court by Benjamin Cyer, Josiah Parrott and Thomas Eggleston.   Will Book 2, page 117   Recorded 8 April 1812

PICKETT, Henry   Orange County, N. C.

      Henry Pickett and Judith Pickett, his wife, of Orange
County, State of North Carolina to Peter Fontaine of Halifax
County, State of Virginia ... cons. 30 pounds ... 160 acres
of land in Halifax County ... adjoining Glidewell, Tindall

and Benjamin Faulkner.
Dated 8 Sept. 1802   Recorded 27 Sept. 1802

    Ref: Halifax County Deed Book 19, page 360

HALE, Rittah (Henrietta)   Smith County, Tenn.

    Know all men by these presents that I, Rittah Hale of
Smith County, State of Tennessee, for divers good causes, me
hereunto moving, do nominate and appoint Elijah Puryear my
true and lawful attorney to recover from any person in the
State of Virginia, all that is due to me from my father's
estate by the death of my mother Wilmoth Averett.
Dated 9 March 1823   Recorded 15 Dec. 1823

    Ref: Mecklenburg County Deed Book 20, page 379

MOSELEY, John (Junr.)   Edgefield County, S. C.

    Know all men by these presents that I, John Moseley of
Edgefield County, State of South Carolina, have appointed my
father, John Moseley of Warren County, State of North Carolina, my true and lawful attorney to collect all debts due
to me.
Witnesses: William Williams and Joseph Moseley
Dated 7 January 1793   Recorded Aug. Court 1793

    Ref: Warren County, North Carolina, Order Book 6

MOSELEY, John et als   Bute County, N. C.

    William Williams of Goochland County, Colony of Virgi-
nia, ... for the natural love and affection I have for the
children of my daughter Anne Moseley, deceased, late wife of
John Moseley of Bute County, Province of North Carolina, and
five shillings, give to my grandchildren William Moseley,
John Moseley, Joseph Moseley, Jesse Moseley, James Moseley,
Elizabeth Moseley, Mary Moseley and Ann Moseley ... slaves
and other personal property for their support.
Dated 2 March 1774   Recorded Aug. Court 1774

    Ref: Bute County, North Carolina, Will Book 2, page 19

Note: Colonial Granville County, North Carolina, was formed
    in 1746 from Edgecombe County. In 1764, the eastern
    half of Granville County was cut off to form Bute
    County. In 1779, Bute County was cut into Warren and
    Franklin Counties, and Bute County became extinct.
    Extant Bute records are now in Warren County.

CLARK, Isham et als   Claiborne County, Tenn.

Know all men by these presents that we, Isham Clark,
Silas Clark and John Simmons, all of Claiborne County, State
of Tennessee, for divers good causes, we thereunto moving,
have appointed our trusty and well beloved friend Joseph
Clark of Claiborne County, State of Tennessee, our true and
lawful attorney to ask, demand, sue for, recover and receive
two negroes plus their increase which are supposed to be in
the possession of David Maize (Mayes) of Pittsylvania County, State of Virginia, and to carry on any business respect-
ing any legacy or property to which we have any claim or
right to in Pittsylvania County.
Dated 6 Sept. 1802   Recorded 28 Feb. 1803

Ref: Halifax County Deed Book 19, page 468

This is to certify that we, Joseph Clark, William Slate
Isham Clark, Silas Clark and John Simmons, of the County of
Claiborne, State of Tennessee, have received of David Mayes
two negroes mentioned in a Power of Attorney.
Dated 24 November 1802

Ref: Halifax County Deed Book 19, page 468

M.B. 7 Sept. 1785 - David Mayes and Frances Smith, daughter
                    of James Smith
                    Surety: William Mayes, Senr.
                    Consent: James Smith
      Married 8 Sept. 1785 by the Rev. Hawkins Landrum

Ref: Halifax County Marriage Records, page 7

William Slate and Caroline Matilda Slate, his wife,
Isham Clark, Silas Clark and John Simmons, who married Phebe
Clark, the said Caroline Matilda, Isham, Silas and Phebe
being children of Joseph Clark and Nancy Clark, his wife,
the said Nancy being a daughter of James Smith, deceased,
late of Halifax County, State of Virginia, but the said
Isham Clark, Silas Clark and John Simmons now reside in the
State of Tennessee, to Gardiner Mayes of Pittsylvania County, State of Virginia ... cons. 75 pounds ... all right,
title and interest in the land, slaves and other estate of
James Smith, deceased, as heirs and representatives of the
said Nancy Clark a daughter of James Smith, deceased.
Dated 20 November 1802   Date recorded not given

Ref: Halifax County Deed Book 19, page 469

M.B. 19 Dec. 1796 - William Slate and Caroline M. Clark
                    Surety: Joseph Clark
      Married 22 Dec. 1796 by the Rev. William Moore

31

Ref: <u>Pittsylvania County Marriage Records, page 23</u>

Note: The Rev. William Moore made return of this marriage
to Halifax County where it is recorded.

Ref: <u>Halifax County Marriage Records, page 118</u>

CHEATHAM, James   Bourbon County, Ky.

     James Cheatham of Bourbon County, State of Kentucky to
Andrew Gregory of Mecklenburg County, State of Virginia ....
cons. 55 pounds ... 196 acres ... on Middle Bluestone Creek,
adjoining Finch, Brame, Hall ... and on Speed's line near
the mill...(Including that part of land which is possessed
by Elizabeth Cheatham and in which she has a life interest
- being the land where James Cheatham formerly lived - and
she is to remain in possession of her part until the time
aforesaid).
Witnesses: Alexander Boyd
William Boyd   Robert Boyd   /s/ James Cheatham
Richard Swepson   Richard Boyd
<u>Dated 6 September 1790</u>   <u>Recorded 13 Sept. 1790</u>

     Ref: <u>Mecklenburg County Deed Book 7, page 627</u>

Commonwealth of Virginia
          To John Waller and Andrew Kinkead, Gents:

     You are requested to contact Ann Cheatham, wife of
James Cheatham, and get her release of dower in the above
deed, as she cannot conveniently travel to this Court.
<u>Dated 11 September 1790</u>
                    /s/ W. Baskervill, D. C.
                         Mecklenburg County

Bourbon County, to-wit:

     Ann Cheatham acknowledged the annexed deed, according
to Law, before us John Waller and Andrew Kinkead, Justices
of the said county.   /s/ J. Waller
<u>17 July 1792</u>   And^W Kinkead

     Ref: <u>Mecklenburg County Deed Book 8, page 323</u>

M.B. 9 February 1784 - James Cheatham and Ann Wilson
                    Surety: John Wilson

     Ref: ELLIOTT: <u>Mecklenburg County Marriage Records,
          1765-1810, page 28</u>

                    WILL OF LEONARD CHEATHAM

NAMES: Wife - Elizabeth Cheatham

Children: Leonard Cheatham, Phebe Clay, Abraham
Cheatham, Tabitha Cheatham, Edward Cheatham,
James Cheatham, Elizabeth Cheatham, Ann
Cheatham
Specific bequests to all children.
Bequest of property to wife for her natural
life. Land where I live to sons Edward and
James Cheatham. Other property to be divided
between Abraham, Edward, James, Elizabeth,
Tabitha and Ann Cheatham.
Executors: Sons Edward and James Cheatham and Henry Speed
Witnesses: Henry Speed, Godfrey Crowder and Elizabeth J.
Speed.
Dated 5 February 1776   Recorded 9 Nov. 1778

Ref: Mecklenburg County Will Book 1, page 275

WILL OF JOHN WILSON

NAMES: Wife - Tabitha Wilson
Children: Ann Cheatham, Elizabeth Pulliam, Mary Elam,
Thomas Wilson, John Wilson, Miles Wilson,
Daniel Wilson, James Wilson, Tabitha Wilson
Lucy Wilson, Uel Wilson
Executors: Brother Daniel Wilson and sons Thomas, John and
James Wilson
Witnesses: Henry Speed, Elizabeth Julia Speed, Polly Speed
Elizabeth J. Speed.
Dated 22 July 1795   Recorded 8 Feb, 1796

Ref: Mecklenburg County Will Book 3, page 315

BAUGH, James   Lincoln County, Tenn.

We, David Cowen and Joseph McCracken, Justices of the
Peace for Lincoln County, State of Tennessee, do certify
that Susan Baugh, wife of James Baugh, parties to a certain
deed 28 June 1820, and hereto annexed, appeared before us in
Lincoln County aforesaid, and the said Susan Baugh, apart
from her husband was privily examined by us and relinguished
her dower right in the said land.
County of Lincoln,   /s/ David Cowen J.P.
State of Tennessee   J. McCracken, J.P
30 December 1822

Certificate of relinguishment recorded 17 March 1823

Ref: Mecklenburg County Deed Book 20, page 219

BEDFORD, Stephen *   Cumberland County, Ky.

        Know all men by these presents that I, Stephen Bedford
of the County of Cumberland, State of Kentucky, have made,
ordained, constituted and appointed James Gee of Cumberland
County, State of Kentucky, my lawful attorney, for me and in
my name and for my use, to ask, demand and receive from the
person, or persons, lawfully authorized to divide the estate
of Charles Wesley Bedford, deceased, of Charlotte County,
State of Virginia, my part of the estate of the said Charles
Wesley Bedford.
Dated 12 October 1807   Recorded 4 Jan. 1808

        Ref: Charlotte County Deed Book 11, page 87

* Son of Thomas Bedford and Mary Ligon Coleman. See, also,
  Emigration to Other States from Southside Virginia, Volume
  I, page 34.

CHAPMAN, Alexander   Sumner County, Tenn.

        To All Whom These Presents Come, Know ye that I, John
Sandifer of Charlotte County, State of Virginia, do make,
constitute and appoint Alexander Chapman of Sumner County,
State of Tennessee, my true and lawful attorney to sue for,
recover and receive of Thomas Dillon, late of the State of
Virginia, the amount of the judgement against the said
Thomas Dillon gotten in the County of Campbell, State of
Virginia.
Dated 20 November 1800   Recorded 6 April 1801

        Ref: Charlotte County Deed Book 9, page 17

CLAY, Margaret et als   Grainger County, Tenn.

        Know all men by these presents that we, Margaret Clay
of Grainger County, State of Tennessee, and James Clay, living west of the Mississippi River, for divers good causes,
we thereunto moving, do nominate, constitute and appoint,
and by these presents ordain our true and trusty friend,
Eleazar Clay, our true and lawful attorney to sell and convey a certain tract of land containing 150 acres lying and
being in the County of Halifax, State of Virginia, on the
branches of Catawba Creek ... all right, title and interest
of Margaret Clay as her right of dower in said land, and
James Clay as a legatee of his father, James Clay, deceased,
of Halifax County.
Dated 9 September 1800   Recorded 28 Dec. 1801

        Ref: Halifax County Deed Book 19, page 174

CLAY, John   Bourbon County, Ky.

     Know all men by these presents that we, John Clay and
Patsy Clay, his wife, formerly Patsy Ingram, of the County
of Bourbon, State of Kentucky, for divers good causes and
considerations, us hereunto moving, have made, ordained,
constituted and appointed our trusty friend Henry C. Burrus
of the County of Bourbon, State of Kentucky, our true and
lawful attorney, for us and in our names and for our use,
to ask, demand, sue for, recover and receive all that part,
or portion, of the estate of Thomas Ingram, deceased, late
of the County of Brunswick, State of Virginia, which the
said Patsy Clay, formerly Patsy Ingram, is entitled to as
one of the heirs of the said Thomas Ingram, deceased.
Dated 7 Nov. 1805   Recorded 23 Dec. 1805

     Ref: Brunswick County Deed Book 19, page 382

M.B. 19, Jan. 1779 - John Clay and Patty Ingram, daughter of
                     John Ingram
                     Surety: Moses Ingram
                     Consent: John Ingram

     Ref: Brunswick County Marriage Records, page 21

ALLEN, David   Caswell County, N. C.

     David Allen of Caswell County, State of North Carolina,
to Richardson Owen of Mecklenburg County, State of Virginia
... 262 acres ... on Beaverpond Creek.
Dated 7 August 1781   Recorded 10 Sept. 1781

     Ref: Mecklenburg County Deed Book 6, page 141

     Richardson Owen and Sarah Owen, his wife, of Halifax
County, State of Virginia to Archibald Clark of Mecklenburg
County, State of Virginia ... 262 acres ... on Beaverpond
Creek.
Dated 14 June 1784   Recorded 14 July 1784

     Ref: Mecklenburg County Deed Book 6, page 385

WILLIAMS, John   Montgomery County, Tenn.

     Know all men by these presents that I, John Williams of
Montgomery County, State of Tennessee, have appointed Lewis
Williams, Junr., of Mecklenburg County, State of Virginia,
my true and lawful attorney to settle my business.
Dated 20 November 1820   Recorded 16 April 1821

     Ref: Mecklenburg County Deed Book 19, page 62

BRANDON, Mary, et als   Lincoln County, N. C.

   Mary Brandon, John Brandon and James Brandon of the
County of Lincoln, State of North Carolina, to Joseph Kirby
of the County of Halifax, State of Virginia ... cons. $500.
00 ... 280 acres of land in Halifax County, Virginia, on the
waters of Toby's Creek ... on the north side of the Dan River ... adjoining William Harris, Peter Cousins and Phillip
Thomas.
Dated 22 February 1802   Recorded 22 Nov. 1802

      Ref: Halifax County Deed Book 19, page 404

   Mary Brandon, John Brandon and James Brandon named as
executors of the estate of John Brandon, deceased, under his
last will and testament which was recorded in York County,
State of South Carolina.

      Ref: Halifax County Deed Book 19, page 405

WILL OF WILLIAM BRANDON

NAMES: Wife - Elizabeth Brandon
       Sons - John Brandon, Irvin Brandon, David Brandon and
              Thomas Brandon
       Daughters - None named
Executors: Sons John Brandon and Thomas Brandon
Witnesses: Theo(derick) Carter, Andrew Ferguson, Samuel
           Matthews, David Brandon
Dated 26 January 1778   Recorded 17 Sept. 1778

      Ref: Halifax County Will Book 1, page 233

Note: This is the only Brandon Will naming son John Brandon
      of record in Halifax County.

CLAY, Jeremiah   Clarke County, Ky.

   Know all men by these presents that I, Jeremiah Clay of
the County of Clarke, State of Kentucky, do nominate, ordain
constitute and appoint my true and trusty friend Eleazar
Clay of Halifax County, State of Virginia, my true and lawful attorney to sell and convey all right, title and interest in and to a tract of land containing 150 acres in Halifax County, State of Virginia, as willed by my deceased
father James Clay.
Dated 22 August 1800   Recorded 28 Dec. 1801

      Ref: Halifax County Deed Book 19, page 176

COOK, Joseph   Wilkes County, Ga.

      To All Whom These Presents Come, Know ye that I, Joseph Cook of the County of Wilkes, State of Georgia, do by these presents nominate, constitute and appoint my friend Benjamin Cook of Campbell County, State of Virginia, my true and lawful attorney in fact , for me and in my name, to sell a certain tract of land in Henry County on the Grassy Fork of Snow Creek containing 444 acres, and to collect all money due me and to do all things as if I were present in person.
Dated 4 November 1784   Recorded 26 May 1785

    Ref: Henry County Deed Book 3, page 124

FRANKLIN, John   Cumberland County, Ky.

      Know all men by these presents that I, John Franklin of Cumberland County, State of Kentucky, have made, ordained, constituted and appointed David Dyer of Henry County, State of Virginia, my true and lawful attorney, for me and in my name but for my use, to ask, demand, sue for, recover and to receive all that portion due me from the estate of Richard Stone, deceased, and to do all things as if I were present in person.
Dated 19 November 1825   Recorded 19 Nov. 1825

    Ref: Henry County Deed Book 10, page 175

CUNNINGHAM, Robert M.   Hempstead County, Ark.

      Robert M. Cunningham and Eliza F. Cunningham, his wife, of the County of Hempstead, Territory of Arkansas, to Thomas Puryear of Mecklenburg County, State of Virginia ..... cons. $1,250.00 receipt in hand which is hereby acknowledged, and on payment of $1,250.00 more on 1 October 1836 .... bargains grants and sells to the said Thomas Puryear ... 740 acres on Allens Creek ... being the whole tract platted by Daniel Middaugh, Surveyor, except 4 acres conveyed to Robert R. Rodgers and 1 acre with mill site.
                /s/ Ro. M. Cunningham
                    Eliza F. Cunningham
Dated 20 June 1836   Recorded 15 Aug. 1836

    Ref: Mecklenburg County Deed Book 26, page 611

M.B. 22 Sept. 1829 - Robert M. Cunningham and Eliza F. Boyd
             Surety: Alexander Boyd

    Ref: ELLIOTT: Mecklenburg County Marriage Records,
              1811-1853, page 45

DAILEY, Edmund   Bourbon County, Ky.

   Know all men by these presents that I, Edmund Dailey of
Bourbon County, State of Kentucky, do hereby appoint my trusty friend William Williams of Brunswick County, State of
Virginia, my true and lawful attorney in fact, for me and in
my name and place, to bargain, sell and deliver,and make a
lawful right and title to a certain tract of land of mine on
the Meherrin River in Brunswick County containing 100 acres,
adjoining George Malone, to him who shall become the purchaser thereof.
Dated 6 August 1795   No recording date

      Ref: Brunswick County Deed Book 16, page 168

DIXON, Edmund   Person County, N. C.

   Edmund Dixon of Person County, State of North Carolina,
to William Dixon of Halifax County, State of Virginia ......
cons. 50 pounds ... 150 acres of land at the head of Winns
Creek in Halifax County ... adjoining Gray, James Brooks,
the state line and to a corner of the land left me by my
father William Dixon, Senr.
Dated 27 December 1802   Recorded 27 Dec. 1802

      Ref: Halifax County Deed Book 19, page 410

   Edmund Dixon of Person County, State of North Carolina,
to Warren Dixon of Halifax County, State of Virginia ....
cons. 50 pounds ... 150 acres on Winns Creek ... at a corner
on the state line, and adjoining the land I have deeded to
my son William Dixon.
Dated 27 December 1802   Recorded 27 Dec. 1802

      Ref: Halifax County Deed Book 19, page 410

                    WILL OF WILLIAM DIXON

NAMES: Wife - Joyce Dixon
       Son - Edmund Dixon
       Daughter - Anne Price
       Grandsons - Dixon Perryman, James Perryman
Executors: Son Edmund Dixon, William Price and grandson
           William Dixon
Dated 29 March 1797   Recorded 27 Dec. 1802
      Ref: Halifax County Will Book 6, page 421

M.B. 20 February 1783 - Charles Lewis and Joyce Price, dau
                        of William Price
                        Surety: Luke Williams

      Ref: Halifax County Marriage Records, page 6

                              38

DRAPER, Solomon   Person County, N. C.

        James Tucker to Solomon Draper ... cons. 45 pounds ....
274 acres ... on Allens Creek ... adjoining Thomas Loyd, et
als.
Witnesses: Parmenas Palmer   /s/ James (I) Tucker
           John Holloway
           Hudson Tucker
Dated 5 February 1760   Recorded 5 Feb. 1760

     Ref: Lunenburg County Deed Book 5, page 559

        Solomon Draper to John Alloway (Holloway) ... cons. 25
pounds ... 150 acres ... being the lower end of the land
Solomon Draper bought of James Tucker ... adjoining Christ-
opher Hudson and Anthony Hughes.
Witnesses: George Fowler
           William Phelps   /s/ Solomon Draper
           Parmenas Palmer
           John Hyde
Dated 1 July 1760   Recorded 1 July 1760

     Ref: Lunenburg County Deed Book 6, page 163

        Elizabeth Draper, wife of Solomon Draper, released her
dower right in land.

        Solomon Draper of Mecklenburg County, State of Virginia
to William Creath of same county ... cons. 70 pounds ... 124
acres ... on the south side of the little fork of Allens
Creek ... adjoining John Crowder, John Hammon(d), Richard
Willis and Alexander Boyd.
Witnesses: None recorded   /s/ Solomon Draper
Dated 6 August 1792   Recorded 11 Feb. 1793

     Ref: Mecklenburg County Deed Book 8, page 267

                    WILL OF SOLOMON DRAPER

NAMES: Wife - Elizabeth Draper
       Son - Solomon Draper
       Son - William Draper now living in Henry County, Va.
       Daughter - Elizabeth Royster
       Daughter - Frances Royster now living in Henry County
                  Virginia
Executors: Sons William and Solomon Draper and Samuel Smith
Witnesses: Samuel Smith and Elizabeth Avery
Dated 24 September 1806   * Not recorded

     Ref: Loose Papers in Clerk's Office Person Co. N.C.

* Original will in files but not indexed in general indexes
  to wills. Will Book in Archives, Raleigh, N. C.

M.B. 12 Dec. 1791 - Joseph Royster and Elizabeth Draper
                Surety: Holeman Rice
        Married 27 Dec. 1791 by the Rev. James Read

M.B. 8 Nov. 1790 - Henry Royster and Frances Draper
                Surety: Joseph Royster

        Ref: ELLIOTT: Mecklenburg County Marriage Records,
                    1765-1810, page 108

WILL OF JOSEPH ROYSTER

NAMES: Wife - Elizabeth Royster
       Sons - Abel Royster, Hardy Royster, John Royster,
              Harrison Royster, William Royster, Granderson
              Royster, Solomon Royster
       Daughter - Nancy Bradsher
Executors: Sons William and Granderson Royster
Dated 3 September 1836   Date recorded not given

        Ref: Person County, N. C., Will Book 15, page 152

Note: The will of Solomon Draper, Junr., is indexed in the
      Person County general indexes to wills, but the will
      is not extant. Heir named in index - Martin Draper.
      Solomon Draper, Junr., served in the Revolutionary
      War from Mecklenburg County, Virginia. His enlistment
      papers state that he was born in Amelia County, Va.,
      in 1756.

WILL OF WILLIAM DRAPER

NAMES: Wife - Frances Draper
       Sons - Asa Draper, William Draper, John Draper,
             .Thomas Draper
       Grandson - John Wesley Draper
Executors: Sons William and Thomas Draper
Dated 25 January 1816   Recorded 13 April 1818

        Ref: Henry County Will Book 2, page 136

BAILEY, Ottway L.   Rockingham County, N. C.

     Peter Bailey of Mecklenburg County, State of Virginia
to Ottway L. Bailey of Rockingham County, State of North
Carolina ... cons. $1,200.00 ... sells certain slaves and
movable property to Ottway L. Bailey.
Witnessed: Charles Hutcheson   /s/ Peter Bailey
Dated   Thomas Burnett
     25 December 1820

        Ref: Mecklenburg County Deed Book 20, page 216

DUNNINGTON, Reuben   Knox County, Tenn.

    Whereas, we Reuben Dunnington and Polly Dunnington, his
wife, of Knox County, State of Tennessee, are entitled to
one-seventh part of the real and personal property of Reuben
Wright, deceased, of Mecklenburg County, State of Virginia,
which was devised by the said Reuben Wright by his last will
and testament, and
    Whereas, we the said Reuben Dunnington and Polly Dunn-
ington desire to sell our said interest.
    Know ye that we, Reuben Dunnington and Polly Dunnington
for and in consideration of $550.00, receipt of which is
hereby acknowledged, have sold unto Smith Palmer and William
Wright of Mecklenburg County the said interest in the estate
of Reuben Wright, deceased.
Dated 2 October 1821   Recorded 19 Nov. 1821

    Ref: Mecklenburg County Deed Book 19, page 270

M.B. 11 July 1798 - Reuben Dunnington and Polly Wright, dau.
                 of Reuben Wright
                 Consent: Reuben Wright
                 Surety: William Wright

    Ref: ELLIOTT: Mecklenburg County Marriage Records,
             1765-1810, page 42

WILL OF REUBEN WRIGHT

NAMES: Wife - mentioned in will but not by name
       Sons - Robert Wright, deceased, John Wright
       Daughter - Polly Dunnington
       Sons - William Wright, Joshua Wright
       Daughter - Nancy Davis
       Son - Reuben Wright
       Land, personal property, etc., to wife for life, and
       at her death divided into seven parts - one-seventh
       part to each of my living children, and one-seventh
       part to the heirs of Robert Wright, deceased.
Executors: Sons William Wright and Reuben Wright
Witnesses: Jesse Dortch and Jane S. Langley
Dated 10 December 1816   Recorded 17 May 1819

    Ref: Mecklenburg County Will Book 9, page 40

M.B. 12 Dec. 1804 - William Wright and Nancy Palmer
                 Surety: Thomas Wright

M.B. 3 Jan. 1805 - Joshua Davis and Nancy Wright
                Surety: William Wright

    Ref: ELLIOTT: Mecklenburg County Marriage Records,
             1765-1810 - pages 39 and 136

ECHOLS, Abraham   * Monongalia County, Va.

     Abraham Echols of Monongalia County, State of Virginia,
to James Echols of Bedford County, State of Virginia ......
cons. 110 pounds .... 150 acres of land in Halifax County,
State of Virginia ... being part of the land of Joseph
Echols, deceased, father of the said Abraham Echols, which
was assigned to him by the Commissioners appointed by the
Court of Halifax County to divide the land of the said
Joseph Echols, deceased, among the legatees.
Dated 6 March 1797   Recorded 25 Dec. 1797

     Ref: Halifax County Deed Book 17, page 358

ECHOLS, Rebecca   Hawkins County, Tenn.

     Rebecca Echols of the County of Hawkins, State of Tenn-
essee, to James Echols of the County of Bedford, State of
Virginia ... cons. 50 pounds ... 150 acres of land on the
Staunton River opposite the long island ... being part of a
tract of land layed off to Rebecca Echols - as heir of
Joseph Echols, deceased - by the Commissioners appointed by
the Court of Halifax County, State of Virginia, to divide,
among the legatees, the land of the said Joseph Echols,
deceased.
Dated 26 Sept. 1797   Recorded 22 July 1799

     Ref: Halifax County Deed Book 18, page 174

CHANCERY SUIT

     Rebeccah Echols and Sarah Echols, daughters of Joseph
Echols, deceased, Plaintiffs
                              VS
                              Abraham Echols, Druscilla
Echols, Hawkins Landrum, guardian of David Echols, Mary
Echols, and Tabitha Echols, orphans of Joseph Echols, dec-
eased, Leonard Baker, guardian of Moses Echols, Obediah
Echols, Rhoda Echols and Joseph Echols, orphans of Joseph
Echols, deceased, and Henry Dillon, guardian for John Echols
only child and heir at law of Jeremiah Echols, deceased,
Defendants.

     Ordered that Jacob Kelly, Ambrose Madison, John D.
George, John Collins and John McAlister, or any three of
them, attended by the County Surveyor, do make a division
of the land of Joseph Echols, deceased, among the heirs in
order that a final decree may be had therein.
                              Recorded at the Nov. Court 1794

     Ref: Halifax County Plea Book 16, page 602

* Now Monongalia County, West Virginia.

42

DIVISION OF LAND OF JOSEPH ECHOLS

In obedience to the Order of Court, we the Commissioners have proceeded to make the following division of the
lands of Joseph Echols, deceased, Viz: We have allotted to
each of them 150 acres of land on the Staunton River and
Buffalo Creek, and to make them equal, we have allotted each
of them additional land as follows:

Lot 1 - Obediah Echols 150 acres plus 12 acres
Lot 2 - Sarah Echols 150 acres
Lot 3 - John Echols, son of Jeremiah Echols, deceased,
         150 acres plus 36 acres
Lot 4 - Rhoda Echols 150 acres plus 100 acres
Lot 5 - Drucilla Echols 150 acres plus 300 acres
Lot 6 - Mary Echols 150 acres plus 100 acres
Lot 7 - Joseph Echols 150 acres plus 100 acres
Lot 8 - Abraham Echols 150 acres plus 79 acres
Lot 9 - Rebecca Echols 150 acres plus 150 acres
Lot 10 - Tabitha Echols 150 acres plus 150 acres
Lot 11 - David Echols 150 acres plus 310 acres
Lot 12 - Moses Echols 150 acres plus 250 acres

                   Given under our hands this 1 Jan. 1795
                        /s/ Jacob Kelly
                            John George
                            John Collins

M.B. 29 Dec. 1787 - Jeremiah Echols and Elizabeth Dillon
                    Surety: Samuel Hubbard

M.B. 2 Feb 1782 - David Bates and Druscilla Echols
                  Surety: Moses Echols

MAR. 9 June 1791 - Obediah Echols and Lucy Atkinson
                   Surety: None listed - Minister's return

M.B. 24 March 1788 - Benjamin Gosnell and Judith Echols *
                     Surety: Jeremiah Echols
                     Daughter of Joseph Echols
                     Consent: Joseph Echols

* Judith Echols evidently died without heirs before her
  father as she is not listed as an heir in division above.

ECHOLS, Abraham T. *   ** Ohio County, Va.

Know all men by these presents that I, Abraham T.
Echols of Ohio County, State of Virginia, do constitute and
appoint Joseph Echols of Campbell County, State of Virginia,
my true and lawful attorney, for me and in my name, to receive all money and to sell all land to which I am entitled
to by the death of my late father Joseph Echols of Halifax
County, State of Virginia.
Dated 28 Sept. 1812   Recorded 22 Feb. 1813

                           43

Ref: Halifax County Deed Book 24, page 170

* Abraham T. Echols probably son of Joseph Echols, Junr.

** Ohio County, Virginia, now Ohio County, West Virginia.

PALMER, Anne   Wilkes County, Ga.

    Know all men by these presents that I, Anne Palmer of
the County of Wilkes, State of Georgia, for divers good
causes, me thereunto moving, have made, ordained, constituted and appointed my trusty friend Robert Echols of the County of Wilkes, State of Georgia, my true and lawful attorney,
for me and in my name, to ask, demand, recover and receive
from my father John Palmer that part of the estate of my
grandfather, Joseph Palmer, agreeable to his last will and
testament due to me.
Dated 8 July 1799   Recorded 23 Sept. 1799

    Ref: Halifax County Deed Book 18, page 211

ECHOLS, Robert   Wilkes County, Ga.

    Know all men by these presents that I, Robert Echols of
Wilkes County, State of Georgia, do appoint, make and ordain my trusty friend Evans Echols of Halifax County, State
of Virginia, my true and lawful attorney, for me and in my
name, to act under the Power of Attorney to me from Anne
Palmer dated 8 July 1799.
Dated 31 August 1799   Recorded 23 Sept. 1799

    Ref: Halifax County Deed Book 18, page 212

BROWN, George   Sumner County, Tenn.

    Know all men by these presents that I, George Brown of
the County of Sumner, State of Tennessee, have appointed
Moses Echols of the County of Pittsylvania, State of Virginia, my true and lawful attorney to sell in my name, and for
my use, a tract of land containing 112 acres ... on the
drafts of Allen's Creek in Pittsylvania County ... formerly
in the possession of Thomas Moore.
Dated 3 July 1797   Recorded 18 Sept. 1797

    Ref: Pittsylvania County Loose Papers - 1793-1797
              Virginia State Library

ELLIS, Stephen   Rowan County, N. C.

    Stephen Ellis of Mecklenburg County, State of Virginia,
to Thomas Webb of the county and state aforesaid .... cons.
80 pounds ... 80 acres adjoining Hudson, Joshua Porch and
Richard and Ambrose Vaughan ... and 12½ acres adjoining the
80 acres which Stephen Ellis purchased of John Webb ... cons.
6 pounds 2 shillings 6 pence ... the last tract adjoining
Richard Vaughan on Black's Ferry Road.
Wit: Isham Malone   /s/ Stephen Ellis
     William Ezell   /s/ Mary (X) Ellis
     Joshua Winkfield   /s/ John Webb
     Ellis (X) Carroll
Dated 29 November 1787   Recorded 14 July 1788
     Ref: Mecklenburg County Deed Book 7, page 308

                The Commonwealth of Virginia

To Matthew Troy, Justice,
Rowan County, North Carolina.

    Whereas Stephen Ellis and Mary Ellis, his wife, convey-
ed by deed dated 29 November 1787 to Thomas Webb, 92½ acres
of land, and
    Whereas Mary Ellis cannot travel to this Court, you are
requested to go to Mary Ellis of Rowan County and get her
consent to the said deed.
Mecklenburg County, Va.   John Brown, Clk Court

Rowan County,
North Carolina:

    We hereby certify that Mary Ellis of Rowan County came
before us, the Justices assigned to examine her, and that
the said Mary Ellis did freely sign the said deed.

Justices, Rowan County, N. C.   /s/ Mat Troy
                                     /s/ David Woodson

Release recorded 8 December 1788

     Ref: Mecklenburg County Deed Book 7, page 351

    John Nipper and Anne Nipper, his wife, of Mecklenburg
County to Stephen Ellis of Mecklenburg County ... cons. 42
pounds ... 80 acres on Miles Creek ... adjoining Joshua
Porch, Langford, Cleaton and others.
Witnesses:
        John Nance   /s/ John (4N) Nipper
        James (X) Nipper   /s/ Anne (A) Nipper
        Ephraim (X) Hudson
Dated 30 August 1777   Recorded 9 March 1778
     Ref: Mecklenburg County Deed Book 5, page 202

EVANS, William   Tipton County, Tenn.

    Know all men by these presents that I, William Evans of
Tipton County, State of Tennessee, have appointed Robert H.
Warren of the said County of Tipton, State of Tennessee, my
lawful attorney to receive of Harrison Moseley of Tipton
County, State of Tennesse, all moneys due me from the said
Harrison Moseley arising from the sale of negroes put into
his hands to dispose of for me.
Dated 2 August 1833   Recorded 4 Aug. 1833

    Ref: <u>Mecklenburg County Deed Book 25, page 147</u>

M.B. 16 May 1825 - Harrison Moseley and Mary Evans
           Surety: William Evans

    Ref: ELLIOTT: <u>Mecklenburg County Marriage Rcords,
          1811-1853, page 116</u>

EMBRY, William   Craven County, S. C.

    William Embry of Craven County, State of South Carolina
to Henry Embry of Lunenburg County, State of Virginia .....
cons. 1 shilling ... 1312 acres of land in Russell Parish,
Bedford County, State of Virginia ... being part of land
granted to the said William Embry 27 August 1770 by patent.
Witnesses: Wm Cowan
          Mary Cowan   /s/ W Embry
          Tshr^r Degraffenreidt
          Christopher Billups
Dated 14 January 1775   Recorded 3 Aug. 1775

    Ref: <u>Bedford County Deed Book 5, page 325</u>

    William Embry of Craven County, State of South Carolina
to Tscharner Degraffenreidt of Lunenburg County, State of
Virginia ... cons. a slave ... 1312 acres of land in Russell Parish, Bedford County, State of Virginia ... being a
part of 2625 acres granted to the said William Embry 27 Aug.
1770 by patent.
Witnesses: Wm Cowan
          Mary Cowan   /s/ W Embry
          Christopher Billups
          Henry Embry
Dated 14 January 1775   Recorded 28 Aug. 1775

    Ref: <u>Bedford County Deed Book 5, page 326</u>

Note: William Embry was the son of William Embry (Senr.) of
    Lunenburg County, and a grandson of Henry Embry (Senr.)
    of Brunswick County. (See: Emigration to Other States
    from Southside Virginia, Volume I, page 69)

WILL OF WILLIAM EMBRY

NAMES: Wife - Elizabeth Embry
       Son - William Embry - Part of plantation where I now
          live ... other property.
       Son - Henry Embry - Land and other property.
       Daughter - Ermin Embry - slave girl
       Daughter - Martha Embry - slave girl
       Mentions unborn child
       Mentions land purchased from Abraham Cocke and sold
       to William Jeter. Mentions land sold Elisha Brooks.
       Mentions land he purchased of Richard Talliaferro,
       and which he agreed to sell to David Gentry, French
       Haggard, William Allen and James Chiswell.
       To wife Elizabeth Embry all rest of estate, real and
       personal during widowhood, but if she marries again
       then a child's part for life*
Executors: David Garland, John Ragsdale, Thomas Edwards
Witnesses: Lazarus Williams, William Hawkins, William
          Borroum, John Childress
Dated 6 May 1759   Recorded 5 Feb. 1760

     Ref: Lunenburg County Will Book 1, page 290

* Elizabeth Embry, widow of William Embry, married (2)
  Tscharner Degraffenreid

M.B. 10 February 1760 - Tscharner Degraffenreid and
                         Elizabeth Embry
             Surety: David Garland

     Ref: Lunenburg County Marriage Records

Note: The will of Henry Embry names grandchildren William
     Embry, Ermin Embry, Elizabeth Embry, Henry Embry and
     Martha Embry, children of my son William Embry, deceased

NOEL, William   Giles County, Tenn.

     Know all men by these presents that I, William Noel of
Giles County, State of Tennessee, have appointed Thomas
Burnett of Mecklenburg County, State of Virginia, my lawful
attorney to defend in my name a suit in chancery exhibited
against me in the County Court of Mecklenburg County by
John Winkler, administrator of the estate of Jechonias Towler, deceased.
     My attorney may settle, adjust or handle the said suit
in any way he may think fit.
Dated 25 February 1821   Recorded 22 March 1821

     Ref: Mecklenburg County Deed Book 19, page 23

FARRAR, Feild   State of N. C.

     Feild Farrar of the Province of Carolina to John Farrar
of Mecklenburg County, Colony of Virginia ... cons. 150
pounds ... 83 acres on the north side of the Roanoke River
and on both sides of Allens Creek. Formerly granted to Abel
Farrar, deceased, by Stephen Mallett, Senr., by deed, and
now belonging to the said Feild Farrar by heirship from Abel
Farrar, deceased.
Dated 9 Feb. 1767   Recorded 11 May 1767
       Ref: Mecklenburg County Deed Book 1, page 397

     Stephen Mallett, Senr., and Stephen Mallett, Junr., of
Lunenburg County, to Abel Farrar of Chesterfield County ....
cons. 100 pounds ... 83 acres on Allens and Laytons Creeks,
adjoining Holmes, Stephen Mallett, Junr. ....
Dated 22 Dec. 1760   Recorded 7 July 1761
       Ref: Lunenburg County Deed Book 6, page 382

FOX, Mary Kendrick   Mason County, Ky.

     Know all men by these presents that I, Mary Kendrick
Fox, of the County of Mason, State of Kentucky, do appoint
Samuel Hopkins of Mecklenburg County, State of Virginia, my
attorney to act for me and in my name to settle all matters
relative to the estate of my deceased father William Fox,
and, also, to handle all matters relating to the estate of
my deceased mother Mary Fox, wherein I am concerned as one
of the heirs and legatees of the said William and Mary Fox.
My attorney is to act in my name and I bind myself to ratify and affirm all of his acts.
Dated 17 December 1795   Recorded 13 June 1796

       Ref: Mecklenburg County Deed Book 9, page 101

                    WILL OF WILLIAM FOX

NAMES: Wife - Mary Fox
       Children - William Fox, Arthur Fox, Richard Fox,
                  Henry Fox, Mary Kendrick Fox, Benjamin
                  Fox, Sally Jones Fox, Johannah Fox,
                  Priscilla Fox, Betsy Fox
       Wife Mary Fox to have use of plantation during life
       or widowhood.
Executors: Wife Mary Fox and John Kendrick
Witnesses: John Kendrick, James Blanton, Lucas Sullivant
Dated 4 Sept. 1783   Recorded 10 Nov. 1783

       Ref: Mecklenburg County Will Book 2, page 36

                            48

WILL OF MARY FOX

NAMES: Son - Henry Fox
        Daughters - Mary Kendrick Fox, Sally Jones Norvell,
                Johannah Fox, Priscilla Fox, Betsy Fox
        Grandson - Arthur Fox
Executors: Sons Henry and Richard Fox, William Davis, James
        Harwell, John Davis, Junr.
Witnesses: John Wright, Samuel Lambert, Isham Lambert and
        Stephen Mabry
Dated 9 October 1795   Recorded 9 Nov. 1795

    Ref: Mecklenburg County Will Book 3, page 311

M.B. 12 Oct. 1790 - Sally Fox and Thomas Nowell (Norvell)
                Surety: Thomas Roberts
        Married 14 Oct. 1790 by the Rev. John King

M.B. 9 Dec. 1801 - James Taylor, Junr. and Priscilla Fox
                Surety: Josiah Floyd
        Married 10 Dec. 1801 by the Rev. James Meacham

M.B. 29 May 1792 - Benjamin Fox and Martha Nowell
                Surety: Young Nowell
        Married 9 June 1792 by the Rev. William Creath

M.B. 4 Oct. 1792 - Richard Fox and Nancy Wright
                Surety: Solomon Patillo

    Ref: ELLIOTT; Mecklenburg County Marriage Records,
                1765-1810

FERGUSON, Polly   Shelby County, Ky.

        Know all men by these presents that I, Polly Ferguson,
formerly Polly Beck, of the County of Shelby, State of Kentucky, but formerly of Henry County, State of Virginia, do
by these presents nominate, constitute and appoint my trusty
friend John Burnett my true and lawful attorney to ask, dem-
and, receive all my right and interest in and to the estate
of John Beck, deceased, of Henry County, State of Virginia,
which descends to me or to my husband James Ferguson, and I
hereby confirm and ratify every act of my said attorney John
Burnett.
Dated 3 November 1818   Recorded 20 August 1819

    Ref: Henry County Deed Book 8, page 153

M.B. 11 Feb. 1793 - James Beck and Rosannah Dodson, daughter
                of William Dodson
                Surety: John Burnett

    Ref: Pittsylvania County Marriage Records, page 17

FINCH, William   Bourbon County, Ky.

        Know all men by these presents that I, William Finch of
Bourbon County, State of Kentucky, do appoint John Wilson,
Esquire, of the County of Halifax, State of Virginia, my
true and lawful attorney to receive the dividends which are
or shall be due to me, and payable from the estate of my
deceased father Adam Finch of the County of Charlotte, State
of Virginia; and my attorney is to ask, demand and receive
of the executors any such property as may be due to me, or
will be due to me, as one of the legatees of Adam Finch,
deceased, and to represent me in all matters.
Dated 17 October 1802   Recorded 25 Oct. 1802

        Ref: Halifax County Deed Book 19, page 394

                        WILL OF ADAM FINCH

NAMES; Wife - Mary Finch
        Sons - William Finch, Thomas Finch, Zachariah Finch,
               Edward Finch, deceased, John Finch, deceased.
        Daughter - Anne Elliott, wife of Martin Elliott
        Grandchildren - Elizabeth Finch, James Finch, William
                        Finch, Mary Finch, John Finch, Powell
                        Finch, Edward Finch, Adam Finch,
                        children of Edward Finch, deceased.
        Grandchildren - John Finch, Mary Finch, Adam Finch,
                        Rebecca Finch, William Finch,
                        children of John Finch, deceased.
        Bequest to son William Finch - land in Mecklenburg
        County on Middle Bluestone Creek
Executors: Sons Thomas Finch and Zachariah Finch
Dated 12 February 1800   Recorded 2 Feb. 1801

        Ref: Charlotte County Will Book 2, page 191

M.B. 13 March 1775 - Edward Finch and Jane Puryear
                Surety: John Puryear

M.B. 14 August 1775 - William Finch and Rebecca Clay
                Surety: Edward Finch

M.B. 31 Jan. 1780 - William Finch and Elizabeth Christopher
                Surety: William Christopher

        Ref: ELLIOTT: Mecklenburg County Marriage Records,
                1765-1810, page 47

M.B. 11 Dec. 1792 - William Finch and Rebeccah Willingham
                Surety: Jeremiah Willingham
        Married 12 Dec. 1792 by the Rev. Thomas Dobson
        Ref: Halifax County Marriage Records, page 25

M.B. 20 Jan. 1780 - Martin Elliott and Anne Finch, daughter
                    of Adam Finch
                    Surety: Joseph Lee

    Ref: Charlotte County Marriage Records, page 40

M.B. 18 April 1787 - John Finch and Elizabeth Farrar, daugh-
                    ter of John Farrar
                    Surety: Peter Farrar

    Ref: ELLIOTT: Mecklenburg County Marriage Records,
         1765-1810, page 47

M.B. 4 Nov. 1793 - Zachariah Finch and Polly (Mary) Bacon
                   Surety: Langston Bacon
       Married 14 Nov. 1793 by the Rev. John Williams

M.B. 5 August 1800 - Thomas Finch and Susanna Haskins, widow
                     Surety: Hillery Moseley
       Married 25 Sept. 1800 by the Rev. Edward Almond

    Ref: Charlotte County Marriage Records, pages 200-289

BRAME, David   Christian County, Ky.

    David Brame of Christian County, State of Kentucky to
Samuel C. Brame of the town of Petersburg, State of Virginia
... cons. $220.00 ... conveys all right and title of David
Brame has in a tract of land whereof the late Samuel Brame,
Senr., died siezed and possessed ... adjoining James Maclin,
Reuben Puryear, William C. Wall, Richard W. Clausel, Peter
Hutcheson, Senr., deceased, and Alexander Boyd.
    It being the tract of land devised by the testator,
Samuel Brame, Senr. - one-third to the widow and two-thirds
to be sold for the benefit of the decedants children.
Dated 25 December 1820   Recorded 17 Sept. 1821

    Ref: Mecklenburg County Deed Book 20, page 225

STONE, Marvel   Covington County, Miss.

    Know all men by these presents that I, Marvel Stone of
Covington County, State of Mississippi, do certify that I
have appointed Stephen P'Pool of Mecklenburg County, State
of Virginia, my true and lawful attorney to demand and receive for me and in my name my share and equal part of the
estate of Stephen Stone, deceased, late of Mecklenburg County, due me from the executor or administrator of the said
estate.
Dated 1 May 1822   Recorded 20 May 1822

    Ref: Mecklenburg County Deed Book 19, page 441

GEE, William O. et als   Williamson County, Tenn.

    William O. Gee and Nancy P. Gee, his wife, formerly,
Nancy P. Knott, of Williamson County, State of Tennessee,
conveys to James A. Smithson of Lunenburg County, State of
Virginia ... cons. $45.00 ... one-third interest in 120 ac-
res of land ... which was awarded as her dower to Sarah
Knott, widow of James Knott, and now due the said William O.
and Nancy P. Gee as heirs of James Knott, deceased.
Dated 12 July 1830   Recorded 9 Aug. 1831
        Ref: Lunenburg County Deed Book 29, page 140

                    WILL OF RICHARD KNOTT

NAMES: Wife - Nancy Knott
       Sons - William Knott, James Knott, Richard Knott
       Daughters - Hannah Bragg, Betsy Smithson
Executors: Son William Knott and William Ellis
Dated 16 June 1820   Recorded 13 Aug. 1821
        Ref: Lunenburg County Will Book 8, page 156

GHOLSON, Dabney   Madison County, Ga.

    Know all men by these presents that I, Dabney Gholson
of the County of Madison, State of Georgia, do hereby constitute and appoint Fanny Gholson, wife of Joseph Gholson,
deceased, and Anthony Gholson of Halifax County, State of
Virginia, my true and lawful attorney to act for me as the
same as if I were present, in any way or manner whatsoever
in so far as respects my part of the estate of my mother
Mary Gholson, deceased, it being the property of Anthony
Gholson, deceased, left to the said Mary Gholson for her
lifetime, and at her decease to his lawful heirs.
Dated 25 February 1812   Recorded 28 Sept. 1812

        Ref: Halifax County, Virginia, Deeds

M.B. 26 Aug. 1779 - Joseph Gholson and Frankey (Frances)
                    Waddill, daughter of Noel Waddill
                    Surety: William Waddill

M.B. 15 Nov. 1785 - Anthony Pruett and Susanna Gholson, dau.
                    of Mary Gholson
                    Surety: Francis Petty
                    Witness: Dabney Gholson

M.B. 25 March 1799 - Jacob Lowry and Patsy Gholson, dau. of
                     Joseph Gholson
                     Consent: Joseph Gholson
                     Surety: James Watkins

        Ref: Halifax County Marriage Records, pp. 4,7,42

GOLD, Josiah   Wilson County, Tenn.

    Know all men by these presents that I, Josiah Gold of
Wilson County, State of Tennessee, do by these presents
nominate and appoint Elijah Puryear of Mecklenburg County,
State of Virginia, my true and lawful attorney to secure any
part of the legacy in the State of Virginia, coming to me
from the estate of my father-in-law, by the death of my
wife's mother, Wilmoth Averett, and to take all lawful ways
to collect the same.
Dated 11 September 1823   Recorded 15 Dec. 1823

        Ref: Mecklenburg County Deed Book 20, page 379

M.B. 3 June 1816 - Joseph (Josiah) Gold and Martha Averett
                   Surety: Charles M. Royster

        Ref: ELLIOTT: Mecklenburg County Marriage Records,
                      1811-1853, page 69

                    WILL OF DANIEL GOLD

NAMES: Wife - Elizabeth Gold
       Older children - Ephraim Gold, Daniel Gold, Mary
                        Griffin, Sarah Griffin, Moore Gold,
                        Pleasant Gold
       Younger children - Elizabeth Gold, Milly Gold, John
                          Gold, Josiah Gold
       Names Ephraim and Daniel Gold as older sons and
       Moore Gold and Pleasant Gold as younger sons.
Executors: Son Daniel Gold, David Epperson (of Mecklenburg
           County), and William Sargeant of Person County,
           N. C.
Witnesses: Peter Griffin, Mary Garrett and Charles Hamblin
           (Hamlin)
Dated 27 May 1793   Recorded 9 Sept. 1793

        Ref: Mecklenburg County Will Book 3, page 176

Note: There are no known extant marriage records, but Daniel
      Gold married (1) Margaret Seat, daughter of Josiah
      Seat. Daniel Gold married (2) Elizabeth (Sargeant ?)
      who married as her (2) husband Thomas Hailey.

      Elizabeth Gold, Milly Gold, John Gold and Josiah Gold
were children of the (2) marriage.

M.B. 9 June 1794 - Thomas Hailey and Elizabeth Gold
                   Surety: Daniel Gold (Junr.)

        Ref: ELLIOTT: Mecklenburg County Marriage Records,
                      1765-1810, page 56

CHANCERY SUIT

Daniel Gold, Ephraim Gold, Pleasant Gold, Elijah
Griffin and Mary his wife and Elisha Griffin and Sarah his
wife - the said Daniel, Ephraim, Pleasant, Mary and Sarah
being the brothers and sisters of Moore Gold, deceased,
Plaintiffs

VS

John Gold, Josiah Gold and
Milly Gold by their guardian Thomas Hailey, they being bro-
thers and sister of the half blood of the said Moore Gold,
and Ann Hill and Elizabeth Hill infant children of James
Hill and Elizabeth Hill, now deceased, the said Elizabeth
Hill being a sister of the half blood to the said Moore
Gold, by Thomas Carleton guardian for Ann and Elizabeth Hill
infants.

Commissioners appointed to sell the tract of land which
Moore Gold died siezed and possessed.

Court 20 March 1811

Ref: Mecklenburg County Order Book 15, page 432

Moore Gold, son of Daniel Gold, Senr., died intestate
and Ephraim Gold was appointed as administrator of the estate of Moore Gold.

David Apperson, John Gregory and Zachariah Yancey returned an appraisal of the estate of Moore Gold to Court 13
October 1802.

Ref: Mecklenburg County Will Book 5, page 120

M.B. 8 July 1799 - Ephraim Gold and Jane Hailey, daughter of
Thomas Hailey
Surety: Elijah Griffin

Mar: 20 January 1785 - Elijah Griffin and Mary Gold
Minister's return made by the Rev. Henry Lester
Note: Elijah Griffin of Halifax County

Ref: ELLIOTT: Mecklenburg County Marriage Records,
1765-1810, pages 51 and 163

Note: There is no known extant marriage record for Elisha
Griffin and Sarah Gold. Elijah and Elisha Griffin
were brothers and sons of Ralph and Susannah Griffin
of Halifax County.

M.B. 19 Nov. 1800 - Pleasant Gold and Sarah Wilson
Surety: Robert Wilson

Ref: Granville County, N. C., Marriage Records

M.B. 2 Feb. 1808 - Edward Tillotson and Milly Gold
            Surety: John Hailey
     Consent: Thomas Hailey stepfather of Milly Gold
     Consent: William Tillotson father of Edward Tillotson

     Ref: ELLIOTT: Mecklenburg County Marriage Records,
               1765-1810, page 122

     Wilmoth Averett, administratrix of the estate of Henry
Averett, deceased, bond $10,000.00, securities Thomas Haile
and William Baker.
                              Date of Bond 9 Feb. 1801

     Ref: Mecklenburg County Fiduciary Book

Note: The name Averett has been recorded variously in the
     records of Mecklenburg County as Avorett, Avory and
     Avreth, thus making it necessary to check both Avery
     and Averett for records on these families.

                    CHANCERY SUIT

     Peter Averett, Jarrott Averett, Leeman Haile and
Henrietta his wife, Rudd Averett, William Glasgow and Sucky
(Susanna) his wife, Brown Averett, Elijah Averett, Abraham
Lewis and Levice his wife and Washington Averett, which said
Peter, Jarrott, Henrietta, Rudd, Sucky, Brown, Elijah,
Levice and Washington are children and distributees of Henry
Averett, deceased, Plaintiffs
                         VS
     Wilmoth Averett, widow and administratrix of Henry
Averett, deceased, Joel Averett and Patsy (Martha) Averett,
infants and orphans of the said Henry Averett, deceased, by
James Hester especially assigned by the Court as their guar-
dian for the purpose of defending this suit, Defendants.
                              July Court 1814

     Ref: Mecklenburg County Order Book 17, page 225

               WILL OF THOMAS AVERETT

NAMES: Wife - Sarah Averett
       Son - Thomas Averett - Land where I now live.
       Grandson - James Wilkins, son of my daughter Sarah
                  Wilkins
       Grandson - Buckner Smith - son of my daughter
                  Elizabeth Smith
       Sons - James Averett, John Averett
       Bequest - My survey of 380 acres of land to be div-
                 ided between my sons Henry Averett, William
                 Averett, Matthew Averett and Isham Averett.
       Wife Sarah - Rest of my estate during her life or
       widowhood and then to be divided between all of my
       children.
55

Specific bequests made to all named in will.
Executors: Wife Sarah Averett and son Thomas Averett.
Witnesses: Gideon Crenshaw and Matthew Tanner
Dated 20 January 1751   Recorded 6 Sept. 1757

    Ref: Lunenburg County Will Book 1, page 196

Note: There is no known extant marriage record, but Henry
      Averett married Wilmoth Rudd daughter of Joseph Rudd.

    Appraisal of the estate of Thomas Averett, made by
John Rober(t)son, Joseph Rudd and Matthew Tanner, returned
to Court by Thomas Averett, exceutor.
                                   Recorded 1 Nov. 1757

    Ref: Lunenburg County Will Book 1, page 210

BYNUM, Francis   State of La.

    Know all men by these presents that I, Britain Bynum of
Greensville County, State of Virginia, have made, constituted and appointed Sugars Turner, Junr., my true and lawful
attorney, for me and in my name and stead, to ask, demand,
sue for, recover and receive my distributive share of the
estate of my brother Francis Bynum, late of the State of
Louisiana, deceased, and my attorney is empowered to take
all necessary steps as freely as if I were present in person.
Dated 12 January 1820   Recorded 12 Jan. 1820

    Ref: Greensville County Deed Book 5, page 203

CATO, Martha   Madison County, Miss. Terr.

    Know all men by these presents that I, Martha Cato of
Madison County, Mississippi Territory, do appoint Thomas
Cain of the said County and Territory, my special agent and
attorney, for me and in my name, to ask, demand and receive
all sums due me from the estate of my father (not named) and
all other persons. I herbey invest my said attorney with
full and ample powers to do all acts that I could do if I
were present in person
Dated 25 June 1817

    I hereby assign the above power of attorney to John D.
Maclin to transact for me.
                                   /s/ Thomas Cain
Dated 4 October 1817   Recorded 10 Aug. 1818

    Ref: Greensville County Deed Book 5, page 102

56

Know all men by these presents that we, Judith Goode
and Agnes Goode of the county of Mecklenburg, State of
Virginia, Joseph Fontaine and Mary Fontaine, his wife, of
the County of Halifax, State of Virginia, Joseph Goode,
Edward Goode, Richard Goode, Thomas Goode and John Goode,
all of the County of Rutherford, State of North Carolina,
William Wood and Elizabeth Wood, his wife, of the County of
Greenville, State of South Carolina, placing good confid-
ence and perfect trust in Robert Goode and William W. Green,
both of Mecklenburg County, State of Virginia, do appoint
the said Robert Goode and William W. Green our lawful attorneys to do for us in certain matters hereafter expressed,
that is to say,

Whereas Edward Goode, Senr., deceased, of the County of
Mecklemburg, State of Virginia, died intestate, and whereby
a certain tract of land in Mecklenburg County whereon was
the mansion house of Edward Goode, deceased, which contains
by estimation 760 acres, devolves in law to the parties
above named, and it being more convenient, the same shall be
sold as well as for paying the debts of Edward Goode, deceased, and for the more convenient dividing of the balance
among the parties above, now,

Otherwise the said Robert Goode and William W. Green
are to sell the land and pay to Alexander Donald & Company,
or their assigns, a bond entered into as for the sum of 188
pounds, 16 shillings, 6 pence, 1 farthing, with interest
from this date being 17 February 1796, and

After paying debts and costs of attending the sale,
our attorneys are to make an equal division of the same between the parties above mentioned.

Witness our hands and seals this 17th day of February
1796   /s/ Judith Goode
                            Agnes Goode

Witnesses: Joseph Fontaine
   William Boswell   Mary Fontaine
   Daniel Hutt   Joseph Goode
   Lewis Burwell   Edward Goode
                            Richard Goode
                            Thomas Goode
                            John Goode
Recorded at Mecklenburg County   Wm Wood
Court 13 June 1796   Elizabeth Wood

Ref: Mecklenburg County Deed Book 9, page 99

This Indenture made and entered into by Robert Goode
and William W. Green, of the County of Mecklenburg, State
of Virginia, under Power of Attorney from Judith Goode and
Agnes Goode of Mecklenburg County, State of Virginia, Joseph
Fontaine and Mary, his wife, of Halifax County, State of

Virginia, Joseph Goode, Edward Goode, Richard Goode, Thomas
Goode and John Goode of the County of Rutherford, State of
North Carolina, and William Wood and Elizabeth, his wife, of
Greenville County, State of South Carolina, heirs of Edward
Goode, the elder, of Mecklenburg County, State of Virginia,
deceased,

In consideration of 350 pounds, receipt of which is
hereby acknowledged, conveys to David Holmes and John Holmes
of Mecklenburg County that tract of land containing 768
acres in Mecklenburg County where Edward Goode, deceased,
formerly lived, bounded by the lines of John Hudson, Nevin
Stewart, William Boswell, Hugh Barry, Thomas Massey, Wilson,
Drury Andrews, Cluverius Coleman and Roger Atkinson, together with all improvements.

Witnesses: /s/ Robt. Goode
   Lewis Burwell   William Wills Green
   Abraham Green
   Alex^r Saylor
   John Wilson

Dated 17 May 1796   Recorded 13 June 1796

    Ref: Mecklenburg County Deed Book 9, page 100

GRAVES, John   Fayette County, Ky.

    Know all men by these presents that I, John Graves of
the County of Fayette, State of Kentucky, do nominate and
appoint my friend James Parberry of Franklin County, State
of Virginia, my attorney to recover the sum of 40 pounds
from the estate of William Graves, my deceased father, with
interest to date of recovery, and to give a receipt for the
same whenever a division is made of the estate of the said
William Graves among his children.

Dated 27 June 1799   Recorded 30 Sept. 1799

    Ref: Henry County Deed Book 6, page 189

WILL OF WILLIAM GRAVES

NAMES: Wife - Mary Graves
      Son: Thomas Graves - Daughter: Polly Graves -
      Daughter: Sally Graves - Daughter: Betsy Graves -
      Daughter: Nancy Parberry - Son: John Graves - Son:
      William Graves
      Susannah Martin - connection not stated
      Bequests to all named - Land and all other property
      to wife Mary Graves for her natural life, and at her
      decease property to be divided between all children
Executors: Son Thomas Graves and Joseph Anthony

Dated 12 May 1790   Recorded: No date given

    Ref: Henry County Will Book 1, page 203

HAMILTON, Joseph   Union District, S. C.

    Know all men by these presents that I, Joseph Hamilton
of Union District, South Carolina, have made, ordained, constituted and appointed my brother-in-law Wilson Gee of
Lunenburg County, State of Virginia, my true and lawful attorney, for me and in my name, to ask, demand and receive of
John Gee, executor of the estate of James Gee, deceased, all
that fell to my wife Nancy, by her mother Parthany Parham,
being one of the legatees of James Gee, deceased.
Dated 9 June 1812   Recorded 22 May 1815
    Ref: Brunswick County Deed Book 22, page 427

M.B. 23 November 1778 - Ephraim Parham and Parthenia Gee,
                        dau. of William Gee
                        Surety: John Maclin
  Ref: Brunswick County Marriage Records, page 20

M.B. 22 December 1808 - Wilson Gee and Rebecca Turbyfield
                        Surety: John Gee
  Ref: Brunswick County Marriage Records, page 169

HYDE, Robert   Granville County, N. C.

    Robert Hyde of the County of Granville, State of North
Carolina, to Tignal Jones of the County of Mecklenburg,
State of Virginia ... cons. 250 pounds ... 252 acres on the
east side of a branch of Butchers Creek ... adjoining the
line of Mitchell and Randolph ... being one-half of tract of
land that John Hyde, Senr., purchased of Richard Stith.
Dated 14 December 1792   Recorded 14 Jan. 1793

    Elizabeth Hyde, wife of Robert Hyde, personally appear-
ed Court, and being privily examined, relinquished her right
of dower.
                                        Court 9 Sept. 1793
  Ref: Mecklenburg County Deed Book 8, page 250

M.B. 22 October 1781 - Robert Hyde and Elizabeth Harper
                        Surety: Thomas Lanier

    Ref: Granville County, N. C., Marriage Records

WILL OF JOHN HYDE

NAMES: Wife - Not named and evidently deceased.
      Children: Sarah Walden, Robert Hyde, John Hyde,
              Irvin Hyde, Martha Wooton, Thomas Hyde,
              Elinor Hyde
      Grandsons - John Hyde Carleton and Irby Bracey
      Children of my late son James Hyde (deceased).

Executors: Son Robert Hyde and Clausel Clausel
Witnesses: Edward Dodson, Lewis Green, William Dodson
Dated 11 September 1791   Recorded 9 Jan. 1792

Ref: Mecklenburg County Will Book 3, page 87

PINSON, Thomas   Clark County, Ga.

   Thomas Pinson and Lucy Pinson, his wife, of Clark County, State of Georgia to William M. Swepson of Mecklenburg
County, State of Virginia ... cons. $470.00 ... 36 acres of
land on the waters of Little Bluestone Creek ... adjoining
the land of the said Swepson, Thomas Atkins and Richard
Brame.
   It being the land the said Pinson received in a divi-
sion made by the Commissioners appointed by the Mecklenburg
County Court, and a part of the land on which Caleb Johnson
resided.
Teste: Bennet Tuck, J.P.   /s/ Thomas Pinson
       Edward Jones, J.P.   Lucy Pinson
Clark County, Ga.
Dated 3 October 1821   Recorded 20 May 1822

Ref: Mecklenburg County Deed Book 19, page 443

M.B. 12 February 1810 - Thomas Pinson and Lucy Johnston
                Surety: Caleb Johnston

Ref: ELLIOTT: Mecklenburg County Marriage Records,
            1765-1810, page 99

ROWLAND, Rachel   Franklin County, Ga.

   Rachel Rowland of the County of Franklin, State of
Georgia sells to Robert Ragsdale of Mecklenburg County,
State of Virginia ... cons. $100.00 ... all her part of a
tract of land lying in Mecklenburg County, State of Virginia
which was willed to Rachel Rowland by her father John Rags-
dale, deceased.
Witnesses: /s/ Rachel Rowland
   Caleb Garrison, Junr.
   John Mayes, Junr.
Dated 31 March 1817   Recorded 20 Jan. 1823

Ref: Mecklenburg County Deed Book 20, page 180

M.B. 10 Dec. 1781 - Richard Rowland and Rachel Ragsdale
                Surety: Henry Robertson

Ref: ELLIOTT: Mecklenburg County Marriage Records,
            1765-1810, page 107

HANCOCK, Douglas   Jefferson County, Ga.

    To all whom these presents come, Greetings: Know ye
that I, Douglas Hancock of the County of Jefferson, State of
Georgia, do by these presents nominate, constitute and
appoint my trusty friend Martin Hancock, of Charlotte County
State of Virginia, my true and lawful attorney, for me and
in my name, to ask, demand and receive any and all legacies,
or bequests, coming to me in the State of Virginia.
Dated 7 November 1805   Recorded 2 June 1806

    Ref: Charlotte County Deed Book 10, page 216

M.B. 5 Nov. 1787 - Douglas Hancock and Molly Harvey, dau. of
                  Thomas Harvey
                  Surety: Thomas Harvey
    Married 12 Nov. 1787 by the Rev. John Weatherford

    Ref: Charlotte County Marriage Records, page 98

M.B. 1 Sept. 1790 - Martin Hancock and Sally Harvey
                  Surety: Thomas Harvey

    Ref: Charlotte County Marriage Records, page 147

WILL OF THOMAS HARVEY

NAMES: Wife - deceased
      Son - Nathan Harvey
      Daughters - Molly Hancock, deceased, wife of Douglas
                  Hancock
                  Sarah Hancock, Elizabeth Jenings,
                  Druscilla Harvey, Susannah Thornton
      Sons-in-law - Martin Hancock, Pleasant Jenings, Isham
                  Harvey, William Thornton
      Housekeeper - Betty Underdown
Executors: Son Nathan Harvey, sons-in-law Martin Hancock,
        Pleasant Jenings, Isham Harvey, William Thornton
Witnesses: William White, John Armstead, John White
Dated 9 April 1812   Recorded 6 July 1812

    Ref: Charlotte County Will Book 3, page 197

WILL OF THOMAS HARVEY, SENR.

NAMES: Wife not named in will
      Sons - Thomas Harvey, Blasinghame Harvey, Francis
           Harvey, John Harvey, William Harvey
      Daughters - Elizabeth Paulet, Druscilla Harvey
      Son-in-law - Thomas Paulet
Executors: Son Thomas Harvey, son-in-law Thomas Paulet and
      friend Robert Jenings

Witnesses: Henry Madison, Joseph Barksdale, William White
<u>Dated 9 April 1782</u>   <u>Recorded 5 August 1782</u>

   Ref: <u>Charlotte County Will Book 1, page 294</u>

<u>HAY, Sealy</u>   <u>Davidson County, Tenn.</u>

      Know all men by these presents that I, Sealy Hay of
Davidson County, State of Tennessee, do nominate, constitute and Appoint my trusty friend Nathaniel Wyche of the
County of Sussex, State of Virginia, my true and lawful attorney to act for me and in my name to sell for me and to
my use a certain tract of land lying and being in the said
County of Sussex, State of Virginia, containing about 42
acres more or less, and my attorney is to act as fully and
amply as I could do were I personally present, and I ratify
and confirm all acts of my said attorney.
<u>Dated 21 November 1806</u>   <u>Recorded 7 May 1807</u>

      Ref: <u>Sussex County Deed Book "K", page 39</u>

                    WILL OF RICHARD HAY

NAMES: Wife - Edith Hay
       Son - Richard Hay
       Daughters - Molly (Mary) Atkins, wife of John Atkins
                   Edith Hay, Lucy Hay, Sealah Hay
       Children minors - 200 acres of land to son Richard
       Hay at age 21 - 180 acres to be divided between four
       daughters after death of wife.
Executors: Brother Balaam Hay and friend Richard Drury
Witnesses: William Grizzard, William Land, William Sills
<u>Dated 19 March 1796</u>   <u>Recorded 1 Sept. 1796</u>

      Ref: <u>Sussex County Will Book "E", page 431</u>

Note: Balaam Hay qualified as executor of the estate of his
      brother, but Balaam Hay died in 1802 before the estate
      was settled and Richard Hay, son of the decedant,
      qualified as administrator with the will annexed.

M.B. 15 July 1791 - John Atkins and Molly Hay
                Surety: Richard Hay

      Ref: <u>Sussex County Marriage Records, page 63</u>

M.B. 8 Jan. 1801 - Richard Hay and Louisa Seaborn
                Surety: Thomas Avent

      Ref: <u>Sussex County Marriage Records, page 100</u>

Richard Hay and Icy (Louisa) his wife, Edith Hay, Senr.
John Atkins and Mary his wife, Edith Hay, Junr., and Lucy
Hay - widow and orphans of Richard Hay, deceased - of
Sussex County to William H. Powell of Sussex County ......
cons. 322 pounds 15 shillings .... 322 3/4 acres on Plow-
man Swamp ... adjoining Bolling Long, etc.
Dated 18 October 1802   Recorded 17 April 1803

Icy (Louisa) Hay, wife of Richard Hay, and Mary Atkins,
wife of John Atkins, released their dower rights.

Ref: Sussex County Deed Book "J", page 162

Notation recorded under deed: In the year 1803, we saw Lucy
Hay sign and deliver the above deed in the State of Tennessee, it being her own act, and the said deed is in order to
be recorded in the County of Sussex, State of Virginia
                              /s/ Peter Rives
                                  Hamilton Hobbs
                                  Robert C. Rives

Note: Sealah Hay, being under age, it appears that her part
      of the land willed by Richard Hay was segregated, but
      sold in 1806 under the above power of attorney, the
      family having moved to Tennessee.

WILL OF RICHARD HAY, SENR.

NAMES: Wife - Frances Hay
       Sons - John Hay, Richard Hay, Balaam Hay
       Daughters - mentioned in will but not by name
Executors: Sons Richard and Balaam Hay
Witnesses: William Grizzard, Thomas Mason, David Mason
Dated 18 December 1786   Recorded 18 Sept. 1788

      Ref: Sussex County Will Book "D", page 518

HAY, John et als   Williamson County, Tenn.

      Know all men by these presents that we, John Hay and
William Bullock, of Williamson County, State of Tennessee,
do nominate, constitute and appoint Howell Seaborn of the
County of Sussex, State of Virginia, our true and lawful
attorney to ask, demand and receive of the administrator,
our part of the legacies due to us from the estate of Balaam
Hay, deceased, late of Sussex County, State of Virginia.
Dated 2 November 1802   Recorded 6 Jan. 1803

      Ref: Sussex County Deed Book "J", page 149

Note: There is no extant marriage record, but presumedly
      William Bullock married a daughter of Balaam Hay.

Note: Balaam Hay died intestate in 1802 in Sussex County.
Inventory and appraisement of the estate of Balaam
Hay recorded 3 February 1803.

Ref: Sussex County Will Book "F", page 313

HOLLAND, Theodosia   Shelby County, Ky.

Know all men by these presents that I, Theodosia
Holland, formerly Theodosia Beck, of Shelby County, State of
Kentucky, but formerly of the County of Pittsylvania, State
of Virginia, do by these presents nominate, constitute and
appoint my trusty friend John Burnett my true and lawful attorney, for me and in my name, to ask, demand and receive my
interest in and to the estate of John Beck, deceased, of
Henry County, State of Virginia, which descended to me or to
my husband Jonas M. Holland, and I ratify and confirm every
lawful act of my said attorney John Burnett.
Dated 3 November 1818   Recorded 20 August 1819

Ref: Henry County Deed Book 8, page 152

M.B. 13 March 1792 - John Burnett and Judith Beck
                Surety: James Burnett

Ref: Pittsylvania County Marriage Records, page 15

HUTCHESON, John   Montgomery County, Tenn.

Know all men by these presents that I, Richard Apperson
executor of the estate of Martha Apperson, deceased, of
Mecklenburg County, State of Virginia, do appoint John
Hutcheson of Montgomery County, State of Tennessee, my true
and lawful attorney to sue for and recover from James
Wilson, executor of the estate of David Apperson, deceased,
of Henderson County, State of Kentucky, all sums due me,
Richard Apperson, as executor of the estate of Martha
Apperson, deceased, from the said James Wilson, executor of
the estate of David Apperson, deceased.
Dated 14 July 1821   Recorded 16 July 1821

Ref: Mecklenburg County Deed Book 19, page 130

WILL OF MARTHA APPERSON

I, Martha Apperson of the town of Clarksville, Mecklenburg County, State of Virginia, ... will the estate lately
bequeathed to me by my son David Apperson, deceased, of
Shawnee Town, Henderson County, State of Kentucky, to be
disposed of by my executor at my death in the following

way: To James and Richard, my sons, and Lucy Royster, my
daughter, whole shares,
     To my stepsons Thomas and Samuel and my stepdaughter
Martha Feagan half shares,
     To Polly Gregory the interest of half a share during
her life to be paid to her annually by my executor hereafter
named, and at her death to be paid to Lucy Royster and James
Apperson equally, or to their descendants.
     I will to my son Richard the interest of my deceased
son David to my deceased husband David Apperson's estate.
     To Nancy Apperson, a remote relation of my late hus-
band, $100.00 to be paid to her two years after my death by
my executor if recovered from my son David's estate.
     Executor: Son Richard Apperson
Witnesses: Archer Phillips and Richard Howerton
No date recorded   Probated 21 Feb. 1820

     Ref: Mecklenburg County Will Book 9, page 109

M.B. 30 May 1778 - David Apperson and Martha Speed *
               Surety: Richard Hanserd

* (2) wife of David Apperson

                 WILL OF JOHN SPEED

NAMES: Wife - not named in will
       Children - Will James Speed, Henry Speed, Sarah
                  Hanserd, Lucy Jeter, Martha Apperson,
                  Joseph Speed, Mathias Speed
       Grandchildren - Lewis Speed, John Speed, Mary Speed,
                  Mathias Speed, orphans of my son Lewis
                  Speed (deceased)
       Grandsons - John Speed, Joseph Speed
       Granddaughters - Sarah Speed, Elizabeth Speed
Executors: Sons Henry Speed and Joseph Speed
Witnesses: Reuben Vaughan, John Brame
Dated 26 Sept. 1783   Recorded 14 Nov. 1785

     Ref: Mecklenburg County Will Book 2, page 130

M.B. 3 Feb. 1779 - Richardson Feagins and Martha Apperson
               Surety: Thomas Pinson
               Consent: David Apperson father of Martha

M.B. 19 Dec. 1786 - John Gregory and Polly Apperson
               Surety: John Apperson
               Consent: David Apperson father of Polly

M.B. 6 Aug. 1791 - Thomas Apperson and Kitty Wynn
               Surety: Holeman Rice
        Married 12 Aug. 1791 by the Rev. James Read

                        65

M.B. 1 Oct. 1801 - Samuel Apperson and Polly Worsham
                   Surety: Archibald Clarke
           Consent: John Worsham father of Polly

M.B. 11 Oct. 1802 - Clark Royster and Lucy Apperson
                    Surety: Archibald Clarke
      Married 12 Oct. 1802 by the Rev. Balaam Ezell

      Ref: ELLIOTT: Mecklenburg County Marriage Records,
                    1765-1810

JOHNS, John   Rutherford County, Tenn.

     Know all men by these presents that we, John Johns and
Mary Nash (Johns), wife of the said John Johns, of the County of Rutherford, State of Tennessee, for divers good causes
and considerations, us hereunto moving, have this day nominated, ordained, constituted and appointed Clement R. Bedford of the County of Rutherford, State of Tennessee, our
true and lawful attorney, for us and in our names, to ask,
demand, sue for, recover and receive all such sums of money,
negroes and other property of the estate of Col. Thomas
Read, deceased, late of Charlotte County, State of Virginia,
which may be coming to the said Mary Nash Johns as one of
the heirs and legatees of Col. Thomas Read, deceased, and to
give a receipt, or sufficient discharge, to the said estate
as if we were present in person.
Dated 16 July 1817   Recorded 3 Aug. 1819

      Ref: Charlotte County Deed Book 15, page 164

MARSHALL, Walthall   Wake County, N. C.

     Know all men by these presents that I, Walthall Marsh-
all of the County of Wake, State of North Carolina, do appoint my friend Pleasant Waddill of the County of Pittsylvania, State of Virginia, my true and lawful attorney, for
me and in my name, to ask for and to receive from Captain
John Foster, executor of my father's estate in Prince Edward County, State of Virginia, all of the legacy and interest due to me.
Dated 24 December 1830   Recorded 20 June 1831

      Ref: Prince Edward County Deed Book 20, page 443

M.B. 27 October 1802 - John Waddill and Patience Marshall,
                       daughter of Alexander Marshall
                       Surety: Walthall Marshall

      Ref: Prince Edward County Marriage Records

66

JOHNSON, Daniel   Greene County, Ga.

    Know all men by these presents that I, Daniel Johnson
of the County of Greene, State of Georgia, do by these presents nominate and appoint Harmon Thompson of Mecklenburg
County, State of Virginia, my true and lawful attorney, for
me and in my name, to give a deed to Robert Boyd of Mecklenburg County, for my part of a tract of land on which my
father, John Johnson, deceased, formerly lived.
Dated 5 Sept. 1807   Recorded 10 Oct. 1808

    Ref: Mecklenburg County Deed Book 13, page 584

JOHNSON, John R.   Wilkes County, N. C.

    John R. Johnson of the County of Wilkes, State of North
Carolina, attorney in fact for Benjamin Johnson of Wilkes
County, State of North Carolina, to Joseph Laine of the
County of Halifax, State of Virginia ... cons. $200.00 ....
240 acres ... being the balance of a tract of 350 acres
granted by patent to Benjamin Johnson.
Dated 23 January 1802   Recorded 26 July 1802

    Ref: Halifax County Deed Book 19, page 313

JOHNSTON, Samuel   Warren County, Ga.

    Samuel Johnston of the County of Warren, State of Geor-
gia, to Joshua Proctor of Henry County, State of Virginia ..
cons. 34 pounds ... all that tract of land patented by me on
the Grassy Fork of the Fishing Fork of Leatherwood Creek in
1781 ... except that part of the patent tract sold to Matthew Wells, and conveyed to James Haley at the request of the
said Wells. The tract of land being bounded by James Haley
and John Cook.
Dated 26 April 1799   Recorded 27 May 1799

    Ref: Henry County Deed Book 6, page 165

JONES, William   Henderson County, Ky.

    Know all men by these presents that I, William Jones of
Henderson County, State of Kentucky, do make and appoint
Francis Lockett of Henderson County, State of Kentucky, my
true and lawful attorney to secure any part of the legacy
left me by the last will and testament of Dancy McCraw, deceased, of Mecklenburg County, State of Virginia, and to do
all things necessary as my substitute.
Dated 15 October 1823   Recorded 15 Dec. 1823

    Ref: Mecklenburg County Deed Book 20, page 380

WILL OF DANCY McCRAW

NAMES: Wife - not named in will and deceased

LEGATEES NAMED

Nancy Shelton wife of James Shelton of the State of Tennessee.

Alcy (Alice) Cunningham wife of James Cunningham.

William Marshall (son of the late Col. William Marshall of the State of Kentucky).

Francis Lockett of the State of Kentucky.

Dancy McCraw - Son of my brother Francis McCraw.

Phebe Penticost - Widow of Scarborough Penticost.

Joseph B. Clausel - Trustee for Elizabeth Puryear, wife of Thomas Puryear.

Lucy Jones - Wife of William Jones (now living in Kentucky.

Lucy Bagley - Daughter of William Bagley of Lunenburg County.

Elizabeth Mealer - (Connection not stated, wife of William Mealer)

Godfrey Crowder

My brother Stephen McCraw

My brother Edward McCraw

Executors: Friends Joseph B. Clausel and James Cunningham
Witnesses: Robt. A. Crowder, Luke Wiles and John Crowder
Dated 21 Sept. 1821   Recorded 15 Sept. 1823

Ref: Mecklenburg County Will Book 9, page 449

LOCKETT, Francis   Henderson County, Ky.

Know all men by these presents that we, James Cunningham and Thomas Puryear of Mecklenburg County, State of Virginia, and William Bagley of Lunenburg County, State of Virginia, have by these presents made, constituted and appointed Francis Lockett of Henderson County, State of Kentucky, our true and lawful attorney to receive for us any property due to us from the estate of Col. William Marshall, deceased, of the State of Kentucky, but formerly of Mecklenburg County, State of Virginia.
Dated 11 March 1827   Recorded 9 April 1829

Ref: Mecklenburg County Deed Book 23, page 462

M.B. 14 Dec. 1801 - William Jones and Lucy Lockett, daughter
                    of Abner Lockett
                    Surety: James Wilson
      Married 15 Dec. 1801 by the Rev. William Richards

M.B. 17 Dec. 1803 - William Marshall and Rebecah Evans
                    Surety: Matthew Evans

M.B. 10 July 1809 - James Cunningham and Alice Marshall
Surety: Robert Marshall
Married 22 July 1809 by the Rev. William Richards

M.B. 12 Feb. 1810 - James Shelton and Nancy Marshall
Surety: Phillip Lockett
Married 14 Feb. 1810 by the Rev. William Richards

M.B. 8 March 1802 - Francis Lockett and Martha Goode Marshall
daughter of William Marshall
Surety: Valentine McCutcheon

M.B. 8 Feb. 1790 - Scarborough Penticost and Phebe Lockett
Surety: Daniel D. Watkins
Married 18 Feb. 1790 by the Rev. John Williams

M.B. 13 May 1805 - Thomas Puryear and Elizabeth Marshall
Surety: Francis Lockett
Married 23 May 1805 by the Rev. William Richards

M.B. 9 Nov. 1807 - William Mealer and Elizabeth P. Puryear
Surety: Thomas Lewis

Note: All of the foregoing marriage bonds are of record in
Mecklenburg County.

Ref: ELLIOTT: Mecklenburg County Marriage Records,
1765-1810

WILL OF ABNER LOCKETT

NAMES: Wife - Anne Lockett
Children - Thomas Lockett, Francis Lockett, Phillip
Lockett, Phebe Lockett, Nancy Lockett,
Lucy Lockett
Estate to be kept together until son Francis Lockett
reaches age 20 years. The one-third of the estate
to wife Anne Lockett for life.
Executors: Wife Anne Lockett and William Marshall
Witnesses: Arthur Moody, Caleb Johnson, Phebe Lockett and
Phebe McCraw
Dated 26 Nov. 1789   Recorded 8 Feb. 1790

Ref: Mecklenburg County Will Book 3, page 39

M.B. 13 Feb. 1792 - Robert Hester and Nancy Lockett
Surety: John Wilson
Married 28 Feb. 1792 by the Rev. James Read

Ref: ELLIOTT: Mecklenburg County Marriage Records,
1765-1810, page 62

MARRIAGE AGREEMENT

Between Joseph Gooch of Granville County, State of North Carolina, and Anne Lockett, widow and relict of Abner Lockett, of Mecklenburg County, State of Virginia.

Joseph Gooch is to claim no part of the estate of Anne Lockett, and Anne Lockett will claim no part of the estate of Joseph Gooch except what he may devise to her.

Ann Lockett relinguished all dower right in the estate of Joseph Gooch.

Dated 27 June 1794   Recorded 13 Oct. 1794

Ref: Mecklenburg County Deed Book 8, page 463

M.B. 27 June 1794 - Joseph Gooch and Anne Lockett
Surety: William Marshall

Ref: ELLIOTT: Mecklenburg County Marriage Records,
1765-1810, page 51

CHANCERY SUIT

Thomas Lockett, Lucy Lockett, Scarborough Penticost and Phebe his wife, Phillip Lockett and Francis Lockett, which said Phillip and Francis are infants and orphans of Abner Lockett, deceased, by Thomas Lockett their guardian, and Robert Hester, administrator of the estate of Nancy Hester, deceased, who was one of the children of Abner Lockett, deceased, Plaintiffs

Vs

William Marshall, Executor, and Joseph Gooch and Anne his wife, also executors of the estate of Abner Lockett, deceased.

Suit to divide slaves and money in the estate.
Court October 1804

Ref: Mecklenburg County Order Book 12, page 261

WILL OF THOMAS LOCKETT

NAMES: Wife - Judith Lockett
Sons - Stephen Lockett, Abner Lockett, Jacob Lockett, James Lockett, David Lockett
Last three sons above under age.
Daughters - Martha Bass, Lucy Stone, Elizabeth Lockett, Mary Gipson
Executors: Sons Stephen Lockett and Abner Lockett and Arthur Moseley
Witnesses: Gideon Lockett, John Gipson, Robert Haskins

Dated 8 September 1770   Recorded 23 Jan. 1775

Ref: Cumberland County Will Book 2, page 165

NOTE: Abner Lockett married Anne Marshall daughter of
     William Marshall of Henrico County and his (1) wife
     Anne (not known).

Robert, son of William and Anne Marshall, born 23 December
     1729.
Elizabeth, daughter of William and Anne Marshall, born 13
     July 1731.
Anne, daughter of William and Anne Marshall, born 28 January
     1733.

     Ref: Bristol Parish Register, pages 338, 339, 340

NOTE: There was a fourth child - John Marshall - born of
     this (1) marriage as disclosed by the will of William
     Marshall which provided that children John Marshall,
     Elizabeth Marshall and Anne Marshall were not to share
     in certain parts of his estate. Robert Marshall had
     died, evidently, as he is not named in this will.

                  WILL OF WILLIAM MARSHALL

NAMES: Wife - Lucy Marshall
       Sons - John Marshall, William Marshall
       Provision: My three children John, Elizabeth and Anne
       shall not share in certain property (specified).
       All of my estate not transferred to be divided equal-
       ly between my ten children: John, William, Elizabeth,
       Anne, Phebe, Mary, Judith, Sarah, Martha and
       Susanah.
       Refers to property which came to wife Lucy from her
       (1) husband.
       Francis Marshall, Edward Bass and George Hancock to
       be guardians of (minor) children.
Executors: Thomas Worsham, William Archer, Henry Moody
Witnesses: Dancy McCraw, Abner Lockett, Joseph Taylor
Dated 2 October 1768   Recorded 27 March 1769

     Ref: Cumberland County Will Book 1, page 444

NOTES: William Marshall married (1) Anne (unknown), Issue:
       Robert Marshall, Elizabeth Marshall, Anne Marshall,
       John Marshall.
       William Marshall married (2) Phebe (Phoebe) Farmer,
       daughter of John Farmer, Issue: Phebe, Mary, Judith,
       Sarah, Martha, Susanah and William Marshall.
       William Marshall married (3) Lucy (Green) Clay widow
       of Henry Clay.
       The land on which William Marshall resided in Cum-
       berland County had been inherited from his father
       and, apparently, had been entailed by Alexander Mar-
       shall to descend to the eldest son of William Mar-
       shall.

CHANCERY SUIT

Know all men by these presents that we, William Marshall, Dancy McCraw and Abner Lockett of Cumberland County, Drury Williams and John Robards of Goochland County, are firmly bound to John Marshall of Mecklenburg County for the sum of 1000 pounds to be paid to the said John Marshall ...

Whereas William Marshall of Cumberland County, now deceased, by his will devised to his son William Marshall, a party to this bond, a certain tract of land in Cumberland County on which William Marshall, deceased, formerly lived, and

Whereas the said William Marshall had no right to devise this land to his son William ... but the same descended to his son John Marshall, named above, as heir in tail by the will of his grandfather which entailed the land on his son William now deceased ... same now in Court and John Marshall now defending to recover same from his brother William ... which said William, now an infant, has agreed to relinguish claim to said land.

John Marshall is to get entailment docked in Court by an Act of Assembly, and to sell land and to give half of the money to said William Marshall.

Witnesses: /s/ Wm Marshall

Geo. Williamson   Dancy McCraw

Tho. Miller   Abner Lockett

                     Drury Williams

Dated 28 Dec. 1775   Jno Robards

Memorandum:

I, John Marshall, for and in consideration of 772 pounds 5 shillings, paid by Edward Haskins, release all my right in the within bond.

Dated 14 August 1776   Recorded 23 Sept. 1776

Ref: Cumberland County Deed Book 5, page 430

Note: There are no extant marriage records known to the compiler to show that William Marshall married Lucy Goode, Dancy McCraw married Phæbe Marshall, Abner Lockett married Anne Marshall, Drury Williams married Judith Marshall or that John Robards married Sarah Marshall.

Dancy McCraw is appointed guardian to Susanna Marshall, daughter of William Marshall, deceased, and gave bond as the Law directs with Thacker Burwell his security.

Court 8 Feb. 1779

Ref: Mecklenburg County Order Book 4, page 454

M.B. 4 May 1781 - Miles Hall and Susanna Marshall
Surety: Richard Winn
Consent: Dancy McCraw guardian of Susanna Marshall

Ref: ELLIOTT: Mecklenburg County Marriage Records,
1765-1810, page 56

Know all men by these presents that I, Sarah Robards
of Mecklenburg County, State of Virginia, relict and widow
of John Robards, who was the son and heir of William Robards
late of Goochland County, State of Virginia, deceased, have
appointed Bennett Marshall my attorney to get estate in
Goochland County.
Dated 9 December 1805   Recorded 2 March 1806

Ref: Mecklenburg County Deed Book 12, page 417

Note: Bennett Marshall was the son of Col. William Marshall
of Mecklenburg County, and a nephew of Sarah Robards.

M.B. 13 Oct. 1803 - Bennett Marshall and Lucy Wilson
                Surety: Frederick Watkins
        Consent: James Wilson guardian of Lucy Wilson

Ref: ELLIOTT: Mecklenburg County Marriage Records,
1765-1810, page 85

Note: The marriage bond has name of Bennett Marshall as
Burnett Marshall. Bennett Marshall was named for his
grandfather Bennett Goode. Bennett Marshall with his
brother William Marshall went to Kentucky in 1810 with
their father Col. William Marshall.

Know all men by these presents that I, William Marsh-
all for myself, and for William Marshall and Bennett Marsh-
all, have appointed Richard Apperson of Mecklenburg County,
State of Virginia, our attorney to represent us in all mat-
ters in the State of Virginia.
Witnesses: /s/ William Marshall
   Clausel B. Clausel   for self and
   Philip Lockett   Wm. & Bennett Marshall
Dated 2 April 1810   Recorded 20 June 1810

Ref: Mecklenburg County Deed Book 14, page 282

WILL OF WILLIAM LOCKETT

NAMES: Wife - Jane Lockett
       Sons - William Lockett, Benjamin Lockett, John
              Lockett, Thomas Lockett, James Lockett,
              Hallcott Lockett, Jacob Lockett, Abraham
              Lockett
       Daughters - Susannah Ashbrook, Jane Lockett,
                   Margaret Lockett, Winnefred Lockett
Executors: Sons Benjamin Lockett and Thomas Lockett
Witnesses: John Farmer, Richard Lockett, John Pride, Junr.
Dated 5 December 1756   Recorded 5 March 1757

Ref: Chesterfield County Will Book 1, page 253

28 Sept. 1730 - THOMAS LOCKETT, 400 acres on the north side
of the Appomattox River and on north side
of Butterwood Creek.

Ref: Patent Book 14, Page 48 - Va. State Library

Thomas Lockett, Senr., of Goochland County to Thomas
Lockett, Junr. * ... cons. 20 pounds ... 200 acres on Butterwood Creek ... being part of 400 acres granted by patent
dated 28 Sept. 1730.

Witnesses: Loury Clay   /s/ Thomas Lockett
           William Clay
           Nathaniel Maxey
Dated 18 Sept. 1738   Recorded 20 Sept. 1738

Ref: Goochland County Deed Book 3, page 169

* Thomas Lockett, Junr., son of William Lockett, and nephew
  of Thomas Lockett, Senr. Thomas Lockett, Junr., by his
  will 8 Sept. 1770, left this land to his son Abner Lockett

Note: Thomas Lockett, Senr., in will dated 13 November 1745,
      names sons Joel Lockett, Gideon Lockett and Thomas
      Lockett, daughter Hannah Lockett, son-in-law Perrin
      Allday. Named son Joel Lockett, Arthur Moseley and
      Creed Haskins as executors.

Ref: Goochland County Will Book 5, page 90

Hannah, daughter of Thomas and Elizabeth Lockett, born 28
December 1722.

Ref: Bristol Parish Register, page 329

Abner Lockett and Anne Lockett, his wife, of Powhatan
County to Arthur Moseley of Powhatan County ... cons. 350
pounds ... 200 acres of land ... beginning at a corner wal-
nut on Butterwood Creek ... adjoining Arthur Moseley,
Edward Watkins, Benjamin Lockett and estate of Arthur Moseley, deceased.

Witnesses: Benjamin Moseley   /s/ Abner Lockett
           John Moseley, Jr.   Anne Lockett
           William Marshall
Dated 27 October 1777   Recorded 16 July 1778

Ref: Powhatan County Deed Book 1, page 32

Note: Cumberland County was formed from Goochland County in
      1749.
      Powhatan County was formed from Cumberland County in
      1777.

JONES, John J. et als   Limestone County, Ala.

     Know all men by these presents that we, John J. Jones
and Calvin Hine of the County of Limestone, State of Alabama
have appointed John K. Wilburn of Limestone County and State
aforesaid our true and lawful attorney to ask for and receive for us, and to use any legal means to recover, any legacy, or legacies, which may have fallen to us by the death
of Rebecca Wilburn, late widow of William Wilburn, deceased,
and from Henry H. Wilburn the son of the said William Wilburn, deceased.
Witness: /s/ John J. Jones
    William E. Adams   Calvin Hine
Dated 3 October 1825   Recorded 5 Jan. 1826

    Ref: Sussex County Deed Book "O", page 392

LOVE, Elizabeth   Madison County, Ala.

     Know all men by these presents that we, Elizabeth Love
and James Wilburn of Madison County, State of Alabama, have
appointed John K. Wilburn of Limestone County, State of Alabama, our true and lawful attorney to collect any legacy or
legacies which may have fallen to us by the death of Rebecca
Wilburn, the late widow of William Wilburn, deceased, and
Henry H. Wilburn, son of the said William Wilburn, deceased,
late of Sussex County, State of Virginia.
Dated 3 December 1825   Recorded 5 Jan. 1826

    Ref: Sussex County Deed Book "O", page 393

M.B. 24 April 1798 - William Wilborne and Rebecca Wilborne
            Surety: Surety: Gabriel Moss
    Married 26 April 1798 by the Rev. Henry Moss

M.B. 17 December 1800 - John Love and Betsy Wilborne
            Surety: William Fowler

    Ref: Sussex County Marriage Records, pp. 89 and 99

MYRICK, Howell   Hardiman County, Tenn.

     Know all men by these presents that I, Howell Myrick of
Hardiman County, State of Tennessee, do nominate and appoint
James G. Bell of Sussex County, State of Virginia, my true
and lawful attorney for the collection of all sums of money
due me in the State of Virginia and the State of North Carolina. And he is authorized, also, to pay all just debts I
may be owing and to give receipt for same.
Dated 5 September 1828   Recorded 2 April 1829

POWELL, John   Oglethorpe County, Ga.

WILL OF JOHN POWELL

NAMES: Wife - Boyce Powell
    Bequest to wife - one-third of the land I now live on
    and all movable property for life or widowhood.
    Son - John Powell the rest of the land I now live on
        and land left to wife at her death or marriage.
    Son Abraham Powell - 20 shillings
    Daughter - Elizabeth Bell - slave
    Daughter - Rebecah Briggs Powell - slaves
    Daughter Amey Powell - slave and furniture
    Remainder of my estate not given above to be equally
    divided between my son John, daughters Rebekah and
    Amey and grandson James Powell Bell.
Executors: Son John Powell and brother Edward Powell
Witnesses: John Lumpkin, Parmenas Haynes, Richard Haynes
Dated 15 April 1796

    I hereby certify that the within will has been exhibit-
ed and proven before me by the subscribing witnesses, and
also by John Powell and Edward Powell, the executors named
and appointed to execute the said will.
Dated 29 June 1797

                    /s/ Mat Rainey
State of Georgia,   Register of Probate
County of Oglethorpe

    The last will and testament of John Powell, deceased,
with certificate from Matt Raney, Register of Probates for
the County of Oglethorpe, State of Georgia, has been proven
before me.
Recorded 1 Feb. 1798   /s/ N. Bailey, Clk
                        Sussex County

    Ref: Sussex County Will Book "F", page 94

M.B. 6 September 1780 - John Powell and Boyce Gee (Gary ?)
                    Surety: Joseph Heath, Junr.

M.B. 8 October 1792 - Benjamin Bell and Elizabeth Powell,
                    daughter of John Powell
                    Surety: Edward Powell

M.B. 15 August 1765 - William Gary, Jr. and Boyce Gee
                    Surety: William Heath

    Ref: Sussex County Marriage Records, pp. 9, 26, 68

JOYCE, Robert   Rockingham County, N. C.

     Know all men by these presents that we, Robert Joyce
and Elizabeth Joyce, his wife, (daughter of James Lindsay,
deceased) of Rockingham County, State of North Carolina, do
appoint our friend Jacob Michaux of Patrick County, State of
Virginia, our lawful attorney to collect of Reuben and
Daniel Lindsay of Henry County, State of Virginia, executors
of the estate of James Lindsay, deceased, the proportionate
part of the legacy which Elizabeth Lindsay, alias Joyce, is
entitled to as one of the legatees of James Lindsay, deceased.
Dated 30 July 1799   Recorded 28 Sept. 1799

     Ref: Henry County Deed Book 6, page 184

LEIGH, Walter   Richmond County, Ga.

     Walter Leigh of Richmond County, State of Georgia, to
William Vaughan of Mecklenburg County, State of Virginia ...
cons. 40 pounds ... 100 acres ... adjoining the lands of
James Wilkins, Joel Chandler, James Vaughan, Henry Newton,
Robert Newton and William Hailey.
Dated 8 Nov. 1784   Recorded 8 Nov. 1784

     Ref: Mecklenburg County Deed Book 6, page 416

                WILL OF WALTER LEIGH, SENR.

NAMES: Wife - Agnes Leigh
       Daughter - Sarah Hix - Son - Samuel Leigh
       Other children mentioned but not by name
       After bequest to daughter Sarah Hix, all rest of the
       estate left to wife Agnes Leigh for life or widow-
       hood, and then to be divided between all children
       except Sarah Hix.
Executors: Wife Agnes Leigh, son Samuel Leigh and friend
              Anselm Bugg
Witnesses: Samuel Hopkins, Amey Hix, Major Wilkerson
Dated 9 August 1771   Recorded 11 Nov. 1771

     Ref: Mecklenburg County Will Book 1, page 105

                    DIVISION OF ESTATE

     Division of the estate of Walter Leigh, deceased, made
8 Nov. 1779 by James Anderson, William Taylor and Howell
Taylor, commissioners appointed by the Court.
     Report: The widow and children agreed to division of
proceeds of sales totaling 10056 pounds, 17 shillings, $7\frac{1}{2}$
pence, as follows:

Allotted to the widow - since intermarried with Joel
Chandler - one-seventh part - 1436 pounds 13 shillings 11¼
pence.

Allotted to

Samuel Leigh	1436 p	13 s	11¼ pence
Walter Leigh	1436 p	13 s	11½ pence
Benjamin Leigh	1436 p	13 s	11¼ pence
Anselm Leigh	1436 p	13 s	11½ pence
Edward Leigh	1436 p	13 s	11½ pence
Jacob Leigh	1436 p	13 s	11½ pence

We, the Commissioners, find that Samuel Leigh died
under age and his part is equally divided between his five
brothers and his mother in amount of 239 pounds, 8 shillings
11 3/4 pence each.   /s/ James Anderson
                                  William Taylor
                                  Howell Taylor   Comm.

M.B. 12 April 1772 - Joel Chandler and Agnes Leigh *
           Surety: Nathaniel Hix

* Marriage bond faded and illiegible. Listed in marriage
  records as Agnes Light in error.

Note: Walter Leigh, Senr., married Agnes Bugg daughter of
  Samuel and Sara Bugg.

Walter, son of Walter and Margaret Leigh, born 7 Dec. 1729

     Ref: St. Peter's Parish Register - New Kent County

M.B. 1 Dec. 1784 - Walter Leigh and Patty (Martha) Holmes
           Surety: Samuel Holmes

M.B. 20 Jan. 1790 - Anselm Leigh and Sally Greenwood
           Surety: Walter Leigh

     Ref: ELLIOTT: Mecklenburg County Marriage Records
           1765-1810 - pages 27 and 80

LIGON, Blackmon   Greenville County, S. C.

     Blackmon Ligon of Greenville County, State of South
Carolina ... to Joseph Ligon of Halifax County, State of
Virginia ... cons. 200 pounds ....   acres on
Browns and Wades Creeks.
Dated 26 Jan. 1795   Recorded 26 Jan. 1795

     Ref: Halifax County Deed Book 16, page 307

M.B. 17 Jan. 1782 - Blackman Ligon and Elizabeth Townes
Surety: Henry Townes

Ref: Halifax County Marriage Records, page 6

WILL OF JOSEPH LIGON

NAMES: Wife - Judith Ligon
Son - Blackmon Ligon (now in the army *)
Sons - Joseph Ligon, John Ligon, Thomas Ligon, James
Ligon, Obadiah Ligon, Henry Ligon
Sons under age.
Executors: Wife Judith Ligon, sons Blackmon and Joseph Ligon
Witnesses: John Flinn, Junr., Robert Jordan, Elizabeth
Jordan
Dated 27 Jan. 1779   Recorded 18 May 1780

Ref: Halifax County Will Book 1, page 309

* Revolutionary War

LOCKHEART, Thomas   Surry County, N. C.

Know all men by these presents that I, Elizabeth Lockheart of Patrick County, State of Virginia, for divers good
causes, me thereunto moving, do appoint my beloved son
Thomas Lockheart of Surry County, State of North Carolina,
my lawful attorney to receive for me my third of a certain
tract of land lying and being in Albemarle County, State of
Virginia, which was sold by my deceased husband Thomas Lockheart to Andrew Greer.
Dated 16 October 1793   Recorded 28 Oct. 1793

Ref: Henry County Deed Book 5, page 76

WILL OF THOMAS LOCKHEART

NAMES: Wife - Elizabeth Lockheart
Sons - Thomas Lockheart, Richard Lockheart, David
Lockheart, Robert Lockheart, William Lockheart
Daughters - Margaret Tedford, Agnes Slause, Martha
Lockheart
Bequests to sons and daughters. To wife Elizabeth
land and plantation, Negro woman Judah, livestock,
tools and household furniture during her natural
life. Any personal property not given, after bequest,
left to disposal of wife as she may desire.
Executors: Wife Elizabeth Lockheart and George Dodson, Senr.
Witnesses: John Sharp, Robert Sharp, Margaret Dodson
Dated 24 Nov. 1790   Recorded 30 May 1791

Ref: Henry County Will Book 1, page 207

LUMSDEN, Jeremiah   State of Georgia

    Jeremiah Lumsden of the State of Georgia to Isham
Belshar, Junr., of the County of Franklin, State of Virginia,
... cons. 48 pounds ... 150 acres on the south side of the
Blackwater River in Franklin County.
Dated 19 Nov. 1792   Recorded Dec. Court 1792

    Ref: Franklin County Deed Book 2, page 446

WILL OF JOHN LUMSDEN

NAMES: Wife - Wilmoth Lumsden
      Sons - Jeremiah Lumsden, Elijah Lumsden, Jesse
          Lumsden, Dudley Lumsden
      Daughters - None named
Executors: Wife Wilmoth Lumsden and friend Jonathon Price
Witnesses: Evan Price, Obadiah Belshar and Isom Belshar
Dated (no date recorded)   Recorded 3 Nov. 1788

    Ref: Franklin County Will Book 1, page 28

M.B. 7 Feb. 1787 - Elijah Lumsden and Rachel Greer, daughter
             of Benjamin Greer
             Surety: Jesse Lumsden

M.B. 7 June 1802 - Dudley Lumsden and Sally Chitwood
             Surety: John Chitwood

    Ref: Franklin County Marriage Records, page 147

MOODY, William   Lincoln County, Ky.

    William Moody of Lincoln County, State of Kentucky, to
Henry Moody of Mecklenburg County, State of Virginia ....
cons. 50 pounds ... sells and delivers to Henry Moody ......
one negro girl.
Witnesses: Wm Marshall
          Dancy McCraw   /s/ Wm Moody
          Robert Williamson
          Saml Hester, Senr
Dated 8 October 1794

    Received of Henry Moody 8 October 1794 fifty pounds for
the negro sold to him.
               /s/ Wm Moody

    The foregoing bill of sale from William Moody to Henry
Moody and receipt recorded.   8 Oct. 1794

    Ref: Mecklenburg County Deed Book 8, page 463

Know all men by these presents that I, Charles McCarty
of the County of Christian, State of Kentucky, do by these
presents constitute and appoint Benjamin Boxley of Halifax
County, State of Virginia, my lawful attorney to act for me
and in my stead ... to handle all unsettled matters, and to
dispose of my lands in Halifax County, Virginia.
Dated 1 Nov. 1816   Recorded 23 Dec. 1816
     Ref: Halifax County Deed Book 26, page 325

Charles McCarty and Ursulla, his wife, of Christian
County, State of Kentucky, to James L. Blackwell of Halifax
County, State of Virginia ... cons. $1,256.67 ... 367 acres
of land in Halifax County ... etc.
Dated 6 May 1817   Recorded 28 July 1817
     Ref: Halifax County Deed Book 26, page 509

M.B. 22 July 1793 - Charles McCarty and Ursulla Palmer
                Surety: James Palmer
     Ref: Halifax County Marriage Records, page 28

Will of Jarrad McCarty

Names: Wife - Sarah Ann McCarty
       Children - Joseph McCarty, Charles McCarty, Mary
       Blackwell, Sarah Seay, Martin McCarty, John McCarty,
       William McCarty, Elizabeth McCarty, Mildred McCarty
       My younger children - John, William, Elizabeth and
       Mildred McCarty
Executors: Wife Sarah Ann McCarty, sons Joseph and Charles
           McCarty
Dated 4 Feb. 1793   Recorded 22 July 1793
     Ref: Halifax County Will Book 3, page 68

M.B. 11 July 1787 - William Blackwell and Mary McCarty
                Surety: Charles McCarty
       Married 14 July 1787 by the Rev. Reuben Pickett
     Ref: Halifax County Marriage Records, page 10

M.B. 5 February 1789 - John Seay and Sally McCarty, dau. of
                Jarrad McCarty, who signs consent.
     Ref: Halifax County Marriage Records, page 16

M. 9 October 1799 - James Blackwell and Elizabeth McCarty
                Married by the Rev. Reuben Pickett
     Ref: Halifax County Ministers' Returns, page 137

M.B. 30 March 1792 - Joseph McCarty and Sally Faulkner
                Surety: Hampton Wade
     Ref: Halifax County Marriage Records, page 25

HAYES, William   Fayette County, Ky.

    Know all men by these presents that I, William Hayes of
Fayette County, State of Kentucky, have relinquished for myself and my heirs and assigns for ever to my sister Margaret
Plummer of Mecklenburg County, State of Virginia, all right
to the within (named) slaves and their increase since the
year 1783.
    Teste: /s/ W. Hayes
    James Batte
Dated 29 October 1808   Recorded 12 June 1809

    Ref: Mecklenburg County Deed Book 14, page 91

    Know all men by these presents that I Thomas Hayes of
Mecklenburg County, State of Virginia, have appointed my son
William Hayes of the county aforesaid, my true and lawful
attorney to sell for me certain named slaves.
Witnesses: Clau. Clausel
        Joseph B. Clausel   /s/ Thos Hayes
        Richard Clausel, Jr.
Dated 9 June 1789   Recorded 13 July 1789

    Ref: Mecklenburg County Deed Book 7, page 431

PATE, Polly (Mary)   Bedford County, Tenn.

    Know all men by these presents that I, Polly Pate of
Bedford County, State of Tennessee - one of the joint heirs
of Hardy Pate, deceased, who died intestate leaving six
heirs, whereby I the said Polly Pate became entitled to an
undivided one-sixth part of a certain tract of land situate
in Sussex County and Southampton County, State of Virginia,
containing 300 acres whereon the said Hardy Pate lived at
the time of his death - have appoihted my brother Persons
Pate my true and lawful attorney to sell and convey my one-
sixth part of the said land, and to do all that is legally
necessary to be done
Witnesses: William Reed   /s/ Polly Pate
        Samuel Loyd
Dated 22 February 1817   Recorded 3 April 1817

    Ref: Sussex County Deed Book "M", page 182

HARRISON, Footman   Wake County, N.C.

    Know all men by these presents that I, Footman Harris-
on of the County of Wake, State of North Carolina, do appoint John Walker of the County of Sussex, State of Virginia
my true and lawful attorney to sell a tract of land - the

title to which is in my name - situate in the County of King George, State of Virginia, containing 249 acres now in the tenure and occupation of John Skinker, Esquire, the title of the said land having descended (to me) from my father Lovell Harrison, deceased. James Walker, my attorney, may give the said John Skinker, Esquire, the preference in purchasing the land, and make and deliver a deed to said Skinker or other purchaser of the land.

Witnesses: Wm Massenburg   /s/ Footman Harrison
          D. Fisher
          Jo^n Tomlinson

Dated 22 February 1788   Recorded 19 June 1788

Ref: Sussex County Deed Book "G", page 201

MILLER, Bersheba   Washington County, N. C.

Know all men by these presents that I, Bersheba Miller (formerly Bersheba Campbell) of Washington County, State of North Carolina, have appointed Edward Reese of Southampton County, State of Virginia, my true and lawful attorney, for me and in my name, to demand of the proper person or persons the money due to me from the estate of my deceased uncle, Curtis Land of Sussex County, State of Virginia, and to take all steps necessary to collect the same.

Dated 20 July 1821   Recorded 1 Nov. 1821

Ref: Sussex County Deed Book "N", page 274

WILL OF CURTIS LAND, SENR.

NAMES: Wife - Priscilla Land
      Sons - Bird Land, Curtis Land, William Land, Charles Land.
      Daughters - Elizabeth Joiner, Rebecca Campbell, Winifred Hutchins, Mildred Land, Priscilla Land, Ruth Land

Executor: Son Curtis Land
Witnesses: Joseph Renn, Webb Land, Henry Freeman, Junr.
Dated 17 November 1771   Recorded 15 May 1783

Ref: Sussex County Will Book "D", page 153

M.B. 23 Nov. 1786 - Charles Land and Mary Cooper
           Minister's Return of Rev. John Meglamore

M.B. 20 December 1787 - Cary Magee and Ruth Land
           Surety: John Magee

Ref: Sussex County Marriage Records, pp. 49 and 260

MARR, William   Davidson County, Tenn.

     Know all men by these presents that I, William Marr, of
Davidson County, State of Tennessee, have bargained and sold
to Constant Hardiman all interest, right and title I have to
a tract of land in Henry County, State of Virginia, being
the place where my father John Marr lived at the time of his
death, for the consideration of eight hundred dollars.
Dated 5 Feb. 1818   Recorded Jan. Court 1819

          Ref: Henry County Deed Book 8, page 305

     Inventory and appraisal of the estate of John Marr made
10 October 1793 by William Mitchell, William Hulet and John
Pace - Valuation 1260 pounds 7 pence, including 16 slaves
valued at 635 pounds.   Recording date not given

          Ref: Henry County Will Book 1, page 244

     Estate account of John Marr, deceased, showing payment
to William Marr for expenses to Person County, North Carolina, referring to letters of administration in Carolina in-
dicating that John Marr owned property in Person County, was
returned to Court 1 August 1793 by Susannah Marr, administratrix.

          Ref: Henry County Will Book 1, page 272

MONTGOMERY, Nathan et als   Green County, Ky.

     Nathan Montgomery and Elizabeth Montgomery, his wife,
of Green County, State of Kentucky, to Isaac Coles of
Halifax County, State of Virginia ....cons. 200 pounds current money of Virginia ... 300 acres ... being the land bequeathed by David Lawson to Elizabeth Lawson, his daughter,
by his last will and testament dated 15 November 1774, lying
on the Dan River in Halifax County, Virginia.
Dated 20 August 1799   Recorded 23 Dec. 1799

          Ref: Halifax County Deed Book 18, pag e 264

               WILL OF DAVID LAWSON

NAMES: Wife - Frances Lawson
         Children - Anna Lawson, William Lawson, David Lawson
              Aaron Lawson, James Lawson, Elisha Lawson
              Elizabeth Lawson
Executors: Wife Frances Lawson, John Lawson, John Armstrong
Dated 15 November 1774   Recorded 16 Feb. 1775

          Ref: Halifax County Will Book 1, page 104

                              84

MOODY, Francis   Maury County, Tenn.

   Know all men by these presents that I, Francis Moody of
Maury County, State of Tennessee, have by these presents ap-
pointed and ordained William Knott of Mecklenburg County,
State of Virginia, my true and lawful attorney to transact
any business for me, and to receive any money due to me.
Dated 28 April 1818   Recorded 19 Aug. 1818

      Ref: Mecklenburg County Deed Book 17, page 424

HOLLOWAY, John   Henderson County, Ky.

   Know all men by these presents that I, John Holloway of
Henderson County, State of Kentucky, have appointed my good
friend Charles Baskervill of Mecklenburg County, State of
Virginia, my true and lawful attorney to apply for and to
receive all monies due me in the State of Virginia, and to
handle all matters (for me) as I would myself.
Dated 17 September 1818   Recorded 17 Nov. 1818

      Ref: Mecklenburg County Deed Book 17, page 488

WILSON, James   Henderson County, Ky.

   Know all men by these presents that we, John R. Lucas
and Rebecca W. Lucas of Mecklenburg County, State of Virginia, do appoint our trusty friends, James Wilson and John
Holloway of Henderson County, State of Kentucky, or the sur-
vivor of them, our attorney to sell for us a tract of land
in Hopkins County, State of Kentucky, on Drakes Creek ....
which was entered and patented in the name of Holt Richardson... and which by recent survey contains 1422 acres or
thereabouts ... and to give title to said land.
Dated 20 November 1820   Recorded 20 Nov. 1820

      Ref: Mecklenburg County Deed Book 18, page 401

HOLLOWAY, James   Jessamine County, Ky.

   Know all men by these presents that I, James Holloway
of Jessamine County, State of Kentucky, have by these presents appointed my trusty friend and nephew George Holloway
of Bourbon County, State of Kentucky, my agent and attorney
in fact to transact business of every description (for me)
in the State of Virginia, and to be more particular:
   Be it known that John Holloway, my brother of Prince
George County, State of Virginia, died many years since
leaving a considerable estate, a part of which is coming to
me since the death of the said John's wife, who departed
this life some time since, now

85

My agent and attorney is to collect my proportion of
the said estate which consists of land, negroes and money,
and I authorize him to do what is necessary by the laws of
Virginia, in my name and on my behalf, to obtain my proportionate part of my brother's estate.
Dated 5 July 1818

Lombardy Grove, 5 Nov. 1818
                                    Received the sum of
$228,88 2/3, (being) the one-sixth part of the net proceeds
of the sale of a tract of land in Mecklenburg County from
Richard Apperson, one of the Commissioners appointed by the
County Court of Mecklenburg County 21 March 1815 ... which
is the equal proportion of James Holloway, a legatee of John
Holloway, deceased, and who receives it at the termination
of the life estate of Sarah Holloway in the same property of
John Holloway according to his, the said John, under his
last will and testament recorded in the County Court of
Prince George County, and which is received by me under this
letter of attorney.   /s/ George Holloway
                                    Attorney in fact for
                                    James Holloway
Mecklenburg County:
                    The within written Letter of Attorney,
together with certificate of authentication of same, was
presented in Court and ordered to be recorded.
                    Ed^wd L. Tabb, Cl.
                                    Recorded Nov. Court 1818

Ref: Mecklenburg County Deed Book 17, page 486

        John Holloway of the County of Prince George to Bennett
Holloway of the County of Mecklenburg ... cons. 50 pounds ..
177 acres of land on Church Branch ... adjoining lines of
Mayo, Benjamin Ferrell, William Holloway and line of the
said John Holloway that he purchased of George Holloway ....
being a tract of land given to the said John Holloway by
George Holloway, deceased.
Dated 26 October 1774   Recorded 13 March 1775

Ref: Mecklenburg County Deed Book 4, page 394

HOLLOWAY, George - 10 August 1756: 1063 acres in a fork of
                    Church Branch, adjoining Hubbard Ferrell.

Ref: Patent Book 34, page 108 - Va. State Library

WILL OF GEORGE HOLLOWAY

NAMES: Wife - not named in will and deceased
       Son - William Holloway - 177 acres of land
       Son - Bennett Holloway - 177 acres of land

Son - John Holloway - 177 acres of land
Son - James Holloway - 177 acres of land
Son - George Holloway - 177 acres of land
Son - Thomas Holloway - 177 acres of land
John Speed, John Ballard, George Farrar and Henry
Delony, or any two of them, to divide land for sons.
Daughters - Diannah Holloway, Ann Holloway
Specific bequests made to each of the children
Executors: Son Bennett Holloway and Henry Delony
Witnesses: John Speed, John Ballard, Joseph Dobson
Dated 6 July 1759   Recorded 7 Aug. 1759

Ref: Lunenburg County Will Book 1, page 264

The last will and testament of George Holloway, dec-
eased, was presented in Court by Henry Delony and Bennett
Holloway, executors, named therein.
On Motion of the said executors, who gave bond as the
Law directs with John Ballard and John Speed their securi-
ties, certificate is granted for obtaining probate thereon.
                                   Court 7 Aug. 1759

Ref: Lunenburg County Order Book 6, page 17

Bennett Holloway is appointed guardian for Thomas and
Ann Holloway, orphans of George Holloway, deceased, and gave
Bond as the Law directs with John Ballard his security.
                                   Court 7 April 1761

Ref: Lunenburg County Order Book 6, page 250

M.B. 31 Dec. 1767 - Edward Cox and Dianna Holloway
                    Surety: Henry Delony

M.B. 24 Oct. 1774 - George Holloway and Anne Hall
                    Consent: James Hall father of Anne Hall
                    Surety: William Holloway

Ref: ELLIOTT: Mecklenburg County Marriage Records
              1765-1810, pages 34 and 65

John Holloway, son of George Holloway, deceased, late
of Lunenburg County ... has placed himself as an apprentice
to Messrs. Theophilus Feild and Son and William Call of
Prince George County, Merchants, to learn the art and myst-
ery of a merchant ... and as an apprentice to serve and
dwell in any part of this Colony that the business shall re-
quire from now until 10 October 1764.
Dated 10 August 1761   Recorded 6 Oct. 1761

Ref: ELLIOTT: EARLY SETTLERS, Mecklenburg County,
              Virginia, page 77

MOODY, Francis   Limestone County, Ala.

Granville County,
State of North Carolina:

    Know all men by these presents that I, Francis Moody of
the County of Limestone, State of Alabama, have appointed
Benjamin Moody of the County of Granville, State of North
Carolina, my true and lawful attorney to handle and settle
all of my business in the State of Virginia ... and I hereby
revoke a former power of attorney made by me to William R.
Farley.
Dated 7 October 1825   Recorded 17 July 1826

    Ref: Mecklenburg County Deed Book 22, page 144

M.B. 26 December 1805 - Francis Moody and Anna Hester
                        Surety: Harwood Jones
        Consent: James Hester father of Anna Hester

    Ref: ELLIOTT: Mecklenburg County Marriage Records,
                1765-1810, page 89

M.B. 15 Novemner 1813 - Benjamin Moody and Dolly Yancey
                        Surety: William Moody
        Consent: Mary Yancey mother of Dolly Yancey
Married 16 Nov. 1813 by the Rev. William Richards

    Ref: ELLIOTT: Mecklenburg County Marriage Records,
                1811-1853, page 113

ALEXANDER, William   Smith County, Tenn.

    Know all men by these presents that I, William Alexan-
der of Smith County, State of Tennessee, administrator and
guardian to the heirs of William Glasgow, deceased, of Smith
County, State of Tennessee, do appoint Elijah Puryear of
Mecklenburg County, State of Virginia, my lawful attorney,
for me and as administrator and guardian, to ask and demand
from the executor or administrator of the estates of Henry
Averett and his wife Wilmoth Averett, both deceased, of
Mecklenburg County, State of Virginia, or any other person
or persons who might have money or property due to the said
William Alexander as the administrator and guardian of the
heirs of William Glasgow, deceased. Elijah Puryear is hereby authorized to receive any money and to give receipt for
me.
Dated 5 November 1821   Recorded 15 April 1822
    Ref: Mecklenburg County Deed Book 19, page 418

Note: William Glasgow married Susanna Averett (M.B. 1 Feb.
      1800) daughter of Henry and Wilmoth Averett.

MOSS, William   Fairfield County, S. C.

     Know all men by these presents that I, William Moss of
Fairfield County, State of South Carolina, do appoint Thomas
Moss of Mecklenburg County, State of Virginia, my true and
lawful attorney to recover all monies due me from the estate
of Joshua Moss, deceased, which may be due me as a legatee
of the said Joshua Moss.
Dated 12 Feb. 1813

    Ref: Mecklenburg County Deed Book 15, page 101

     Robert Munford of Mecklenburg County to Joshua Moss of
Mecklenburg County ... cons. 200 pounds ... 360 acres on
Little Creek together with the grist mill purchased by
Robert Munford of Daniel Gorre.
Witnesses: None recorded   /s/ R^t Munford
Dated 13 October 1777   Recorded 13 Oct. 1777

    Ref: Mecklenburg County Deed Book 5, page 102

WILL OF JOSHUA MOSS

NAMES: Wife - Elizabeth Moss
      Son - John Moss, deceased
      Daughters - Patsy O'briant, Elizabeth Cocke
      Sons - William Moss, Wiley Moss, Thomas Moss, Bracie
          Moss, Edmund Moss, Lewis Moss
      To wife Elizabeth Moss all of my estate both real
      and personal during her widowhood or natural life,
      then to be divided.
Executors: Wife Elizabeth Moss and son Thomas Moss
Witnesses: Stephen P'Pool, John Cox, Junr.
Dated 14 April 1809   Recorded 8 Jan. 1810

    Ref: Mecklenburg County Will Book 6, page 285

M.B. 14 Dec. 1795 - John OBriant and Patsy Moss
            Surety: William Moore

M.B. 26 July 1800 - James Cocke and Elizabeth Moss
            Surety: Lewis Moss

    Ref: ELLIOTT: Mecklenburg County Marriage Records,
             1765-1810, pages 31 and 95

     Children of Henry and Susanna Moss: Lewis Moss b. 5-6-
1742; Joshua Moss b. 6-23-1744; Henry Moss b. 5-6-1747;
Frances Moss b. 4-3-1750; Gabriel Moss b. 6-16-1752; Sampson
Moss b. 9-5-1755; Edmund Moss b. 12-17-1757; Susanna Moss b.
4-12-1761; Martha Moss b. 3-7-1764.

    Ref: Albemarle Parish Register, Sussex County, page 97

MULLINS, Charles, Junr.   Rutherford County, N. C.

     Charles Mullins, Junr., of Rutherford County, State of
North Carolina, and Charles Mullins, Senr., of Halifax County, State of Virginia, to John Adams, Senr., of Halifax
County, State of Virginia ... cons. 150 pounds ... 197 acres
on Little Coleman Creek ... adjoining Joseph Jones, John
Angus, Joseph Hewell, Junr., and on the road that leads from
Boyd' Ferry to Pryor's Ferry ... being land where Charles
Mullins, Senr., now lives ... which by virtue of and an ex-
ception for life, a deed made by Charles Mullins, Senr., to
his son Charles Mullins, Junr., which was recorded in Halifax County, State of Virginia. Now Charles Mullins, Senr.,
revises the said deed in favor of his son Charles Mullins,
Junr., and joins in said deed of sale, releasing the excep-
tion of a life right in said land.
Dated 23 July 1794   Recorded 22 Sept. 1794

     Ref: Halifax County Deed Book 16, page 214

MURPHY, John   * Washington County, N. C.

     Know al[1]men by these presents that I, John Murphy of
Washington County in North Carolina, have appointed my
friend Robert Jones, Junr., of Henry County in the State of
Virginia, my attorney to make a lawful deed and title to a
tract of land that I sold to James Greer of Henry County,
State of Virginia, lying on a branch of the Pigg River, and
where James Greer now lives.
Dated 1 Sept. 1780   Recorded 26 April 1781

     Ref: Henry County Deed Book 2, page 129

* Washington District now Tennessee.

OLDHAM, Mary, Junr.   Pendleton County, S. C.

     Whereas, Mary Oldham, Senr., John Oldham and Thomas
Oldham, all of Henry County, State of Virginia, Winifred
Nevills and Mary Oldham, Junr., of Pendleton County, State
of South Carolina., have a negro man named George left to us
by John Oldham,Senr., deceased, late of Northumberland County,State of Virginia, by his last will and testament, now
     Know ye that we do appoint Samuel Elliott of Henry
County, State of Virginia, our attorney to sell or trade the
said negro George who is now living in another county, and
we grant unlimited power to our attorney to act in the premises.
Dated 29 October 1792   Recorded 29 Dec. 1792

     Ref: Henry County Deed Book 5, page 7

OWEN, Frederick   Davidson County, Tenn.

    Whereas by the last will and testament of Peter Three-
wits, deceased, formerly of Sussex County, State of Virginia
I was appointed as one of the executors of the estate of the
said Peter Threewits, with one of the sons of the said Peter
who never qualified, and
    Whereas under the terms of the said will certain prop-
erty was given to his wife Ann Threewits for and during her
life, and then to be equally divided between certain children mentioned in the will, and
    Whereas the said Ann Threewits, widow of Peter Three-
wits, is lately deceased, and
    Whereas it is now necessary to dispose of the said est-
ate in order to make the distribution among the heirs of the
said Peter Threewits according to the terms of the will,
now
    Know all men by these presents that I, Frederick Owen,
executor of the estate of Peter Threewits, do appoint my
friend Drury Owen of the County of Sussex, State of Virginia
my true and lawful attorney, for me and in my name as the
executor of the said estate, to take into possession all of
the estate lately in the possession of Mrs. Ann Threewits,
deceased, of the said County of Sussex and State of Virginia
formerly the estate of her husband Peter Threewits, deceased, and to sell the said property by the laws of the State
of Virginia as though I myself were acting.

County of Davidson,	/s/ Frederick Owen, Exec.
State of Tennessee	Peter Threewits, Dec.
Dated 21 October 1823	Recorded 1 April 1824

    Ref: Sussex County Deed Book "O", page 117

WILL OF PETER THREEWITS

NAMES: Wife - Ann Threewits
       Son - Frederick Threewits
       Daughter - Sarah Owen, Jemima Sturdivant, Frances
            Spain
       Grandchildren - Elizabeth Ezell, Frederick Ezell,
            Jesse Ezell
Executors: Son Frederick Threewits and son-in-law Frederick
         Owen
Witnesses: Robert Jones, Balaam Owen, Ambrose Owen

Dated 18 July 1801	Recorded 1 Oct. 1801

    Ref: Sussex County Will Book "F", page 254

M.B. 14 May 1782 - Claiborne Spain and Frances Threewits
          Minister's return of the Rev. John Meglamore

    Ref: Sussex County Marriage records, page 257

PARROTT, Elijah   Chatham County, Ga.

   Elijah Parrott of the County of Chatham, State of
Georgia, to John Link, Senr., of Halifax County, State of
Virginia ... cons. 6 pounds 13 shillings 4 pence 21
acres of land adjoining William Turner and the said Link ...
being part of a tract of land held by John Parrott, deceased, and by him willed to the aforesaid Elijah Parrott and
other children, legatees of the said John Parrott, deceased.
Dated 20 July 1802   Recorded 27 Sept. 1802

        Ref: Halifax County Deed Book 19, page 348

Note: See Emigration to Other States from Southside Virginia
      Volume I, page 93-94.

                    WILL OF JOHN PARROTT

NAMES: Wife - Ruth Parrott
       Mentions his children, but not by name.
       Estate to wife Ruth Parrott for life and then to be
       divided among his children.
   Executors: Wife Ruth Parrott, Thomas Stanfield and John
              Link
Dated 18 February 1777   Recorded 21 Aug. 1777

        Ref: Halifax County Will Book 1, page 181

PALMER, James   Madison County, Ill.

   Know all men by these presents that I, James Palmer of
the County of Madison, State of Illinois, late of the County of Christian, State of Kentucky, have appointed my honest
friend Elijah Puryear of Mecklenburg County, State of Virginia, my true and lawful attorney in fact for me and in my
name to perform the following duties:
   Whereas James Hester, deceased, late of the County of
Mecklenburg, State of Virginia, the father of my wife Martha
Palmer (formerly Martha Hester) has departed this life leaving Martha one of his heirs at law, now
   Know ye that I have authorized Elijah Puryear to receive my part thereof, and I give my said attorney full power
to sell any property, real or personal, and to execute any
conveyances necessary.
Date 19 March 1819   Recorded 15 April 1822

        Ref: Mecklenburg County Deed Book 19, page 417

M.B. 9 May 1791 - James Palmer and Martha Hester
                  Surety: William Durham Watkins

        Ref: ELLIOTT: Mecklenburg County Marriage Records,
                      1765-1810, page 97

PATTERSON, Jarrott   Rockingham County, N. C.

        Know all men by these presents that I, Jarrott Patter-
son of Rockingham County, State of North Carolina, do appoint my true and trusty friend Jacob Michaux of Patrick
County, State of Virginia, my true and lawful attorney and
in my name to collect from Reuben and Daniel Lindsay of Henry County, State of Virginia, executors of the estate of
James Lindsay, deceased, the proportionate part of the legacy to which my wife, Judith Patterson, is entitled to as
one of the legatees of the said James Lindsay, deceased.
Dated 30 July 1799   Recorded 28 Sept. 1799

        Ref: Henry County Deed Book 6, page 183

PIGG, Mary   Smith County, Tenn.

        Know all men by these presents that I, Mary Pigg of the
County of Smith, State of Tennessee, do constitute and appoint Jonathon Bailey of the County of Smith, State of Tennessee, my true and lawful attorney in fact, for me and in my
name, to ask, demand, sue for and receive all such sums of
money as may be coming to me from the administrators of the
estate of Hezekiah Daniel, deceased, late of Charlotte County, State of Virginia, and I ratify and confirm all legal
acts of my attorney as if I were present in person.
Dated 3 October 1827   Recorded 3 Dec. 1827

        Ref: Charlotte County Deed Book 18, page 47

Note: See Emigration from Southside Virginia, Volume I,
      pages 51-53.

PEEBLES, Dudley R.   Lawrence County, Ala.

        Know all men by these presents that I, Dudley R.
Peebles of the County of Lawrence in the State of Alabama,
do by these presents nominate, constitute and appoint my
friend John Robinson of the County of Warren, State of North
Carolina, my true and lawful attorney, for me and in my name
to act for me in a certain deed of trust from Nathaniel E.
Mabry of the County of Brunswick, State of Virginia.
Dated 22 August 1821   Recorded Aug. Court 1821

        Ref: Brunswick County Deed Book 25, page 195

PUTNEY, Eliza, et als   Davidson County, Tenn.

        Know all men by these presents that we, Eliza Putney
and Martha Wilkinson of the County of Davidson, State of
Tennessee, for divers good causes and considerations, do

hereby constitute and appoint Nathaniel Fletcher of Brians
Cross Roads, near Windsor, State of North Carolina, our attorney, for us and in our names, to ratify and confirm a
contract between our brother Anthony Putney and Joseph
Williamson for the sale of 350 acres of land in the County
of Surry, Commonwealth of Virginia.
Dated 18 July 1821   Recorded 22 May 1822

        Ref: Brunswick County Deed Book 25, page 316

PRUIT, Samuel   Spartanburg County, S. C.

        Samuel Pruit and Elizabeth Pruit, his wife, of the
County of Spartanburg, State of South Carolina, to Daniel
Palmer of Union County, State of South Carolina ... cons. 50
pounds ... all that tract of land containing 100 acres on
the branches of Terrible Creek in Halifax County, State of
Virginia.
Dated 26 October 1796   Recorded 27 Feb. 1797

        Ref: Halifax County Deed Book 17, page 95

PETTYPOOL, Sarah et als   Granville County, N. C.

        Sarah Pettypool of Granville County, State of North
Carolina, administratrix of the estate of John Pettypool,
deceased, John Jones in right of his wife Elizabeth Jones,
of the County of Rutherford, State of North Carolina, David
Wilkerson in right of his wife Sarah Wilkerson of Granville
County, State of North Carolina, Buckner Rooks in right of
his wife Fanny Rooks of Person County, State of North Caro-
lina, Stephen Pettypool, Robert Pettypool, William Wilkerson
in right of his wife Martha Wilkerson, all of Granville
County, State of North Carolina, William Pettypool of the
State of Kentucky, Logustine Pettypool of Granville County,
State of North Carolina, heirs of the said John Pettypool,
deceased, and Sanford Dixon, John Dixon, Jacob Dixon, Henry
Humphreys in right of his wife (not named), which said are
children of William Dixon, and William Dixon and wife Agnes
Dixon, heirs at law of the said John Pettypool, deceased,
sell to James Lawson of Halifax County, State of Virginia,
cons. $600.00 ... 140 acres on the state line ... adjoining
the line of David Winfrey.

                                Signatures
Dated 30 December 1803   Recorded 25 June 1804

        Ref: Halifax County Deed Book 20, page 147

Note: It should be noted that the name Pettypool is recorded
      variously in Virginia records as Petty Pool, Pettypool
      an P'Pool, and Wilkerson as both Wilkerson & Wilkinson.

Know all men by these presents that I, Hezekiah Puryear
of the County of Hopkins, State of Kentucky, have by these
presents nominated, constituted and appointed Cuthbert Roach
of the County of Trigg, State of Kentucky, my true and lawful attorney for me and in my name, and for me as administrator of the estate of my deceased wife Rebekah Puryear,
late Rebekah Jones, to ask, demand and receive all right and
interest in the estate of Edward Jones, deceased, which
Elizabeth Bacon, late Elizabeth Jones and wife of the aforesaid Edward Jones, deceased, held up to her death as her
dower in the estate of the said Edward Jones, and of which
an undivided portion descended to my late wife Rebekah Puryear.
Dated 14 November 1849   Recorded 22 Dec. 1849

Ref: Mecklenburg County Deed Book 33, page 195

M.B. 24 Dec. 1821 - Hezekiah Puryear and Rebecca Jones
                Surety: Andrew J. Elam
        Consent: Drury A. Bacon guardian of Rebecca Jones
    Married 26 Dec. 1821 by the Rev. William Richards

Ref: ELLIOTT: Mecklenburg County Marriage Records,
            1811-1853, page 139

M.B. 6 August 1817 - Drury A. Bacon and Elizabeth Jones
                Surety: Thomas P. Pettus

Ref: ELLIOTT: Mecklenburg County Marriage Records,
            1811-1853, page 13

Letters of administration granted to Elizabeth Jones
and Richard R. Jones on the estate of Edward Jones, deceased, with Grief Green, William Jones, H. F. Stokes and
Wm. Jones, their securities, bond in amount of $100,000.00
acknowledged.   Court 18 June 1810

Ref: Mecklenburg County Fiduciary Book

Elizabeth R. Jones, James Jones and Edward Jones, with
the approbation of the Court, made choice of Richard R.
Jones and Elizabeth Jones for their Guardian.
The Court doth appoint Richard R. Jones and Elizabeth
Jones as Guardians of Caroline Jones, Nancy Jones, Rebecca
Jones, Sally Jones and Maria Jones, orphans of Edward Jones,
deceased.   December Court 1810

Ref: Mecklenburg County Order Book 15, page 350

Note: There is no known extant marriage bond for Edward
    Jones and Elizabeth (unknown).

PURYEAR, John   Stokes County, N. C.

M.B. 24 October 1799 - John Puryear, Jr., and Sally S.
                       Clausel
                       Surety: Hezekiah Puryear
           Married by the Rev. William Creath

        Ref: ELLIOTT: Mecklenburg County Marriage Records,
                      1765-1810, page 102

                    WILL OF JOHN PURYEAR

        I, John Puryear, of Stokes County, State of North Caro-
lina, being weak in body but being of a perfect mind, do
give and bequeath to my son Richard Clausel Puryear all of
my part of the estate of my grandfather John Puryear of
Mecklenburg County, State of Virginia, now in the hands of
my grandmother Martha Puryear.
        I give to my son all of my part of the estate of my
father John Puryear, deceased.
        I give to my son all part, or portion, of the estate of
my wife's father, the late Clausel Clausel, now in the hands
of Susanna Clausel, but which falls to my wife at the death
of the said Susanna Clausel.
        All of the land owned by me in the town of Vienna,
Stokes County, North Carolina, and all of the land I purchased of Naaman Roberts (now of the State of Kentucky) to be
sold at the discretion of my executors.
        After payment of debts, all of the remainder of my
estate, real and personal, to be for the sole use of my wife
Sally S. Puryear for support of herself and my son Richard
C. Puryear for her natural life, but if she marries then
one-third of my estate to go to my son, or in any event at
age 21, and the remainder of my estate to go to my son on
death of my wife.
Executors: Wife Sally S. Puryear, brother-in-law Alexander
           Clausel and friend George Hauser of the town of
           Bethany, Stokes County, N. C.
Witnesses: John Doub, Junr., Reuben Stewart, Zebede Pelleter
Dated 7 August 1809   Recorded in Mecklenburg County
                                          at Jan. Court 1832

        Ref: Mecklenburg County Will Book 12, page 478

Note: John Puryear, Junr., father of the above John Puryear,
      died intestate before March 1777 when an inventory and
      appraisal of his estate was ordered.

        Inventory and appraisal of the estate of John Puryear
returned to Court by Joseph Rudd, John Atkinson, Samuel
Puryear and Clausel Clausel - value not given.
Dated 5 April 1777   Recorded 12 April 1777

Ref: Mecklenburg County Will Book 1, page 228

WILL OF JOHN PURYEAR the elder

NAMES: Wife - Martha Puryear
      Sons - Seymour Puryear, Samuel Puryear, William
           Puryear, Reuben Puryear, Hezekiah Puryear
      Son - John Puryear, deceased
      Daughters - Rebecca Farrar, Jane Finch, Mary Puryear
      Daughter-in-law Sarah Puryear, widow of son John
      Puryear.
      Grandson John Puryear, son of John Puryear, deceased.
      Mentions lots in town of Warwick, and land in
      Henrico County.
Executors: Wife Martha Puryear, sons Samuel and William
          Puryear, son-in-law Edward Finch
Witnesses: Clausel Clausel, Solomon Draper, Edward Walton
          and Richard Clausel
Dated 17 April 1785   Recorded 8 Aug. 1785

Ref: Mecklenburg County Will Book 2, page 111

PATTY, James   Berkeley County, S. C.

     Know all persons by these presents that I, James Patty
of Berkeley County, in the Province of South Carolina, have
made, nominated and appointed my friend Jesse Patty of Pittsylvania County, Colony of Virginia, my lawful attorney to
receive for me and in my name that money or tobacco due to
me in the Colony of Virginia, to convey for me a certain
tract of land left to me by the last will and testament of
James Patty, deceased, said land being on Nixes Creek in the
County of Pittsylvania.
Dated 16 December 1768   Recorded 28 Dec. 1769

Ref: Pittsylvania County Loose Papers - 1767-1770
Virginia State Library

PATTY, Charles   Berkeley County, S. C.

     Charles Patty of the County of Berkeley in the Province
of South Carolina, to John Henry of the County of Pittsylvania, Colony of Virginia ... cons. 26 pounds ... 130 acres
on both sides of Nixes Creek ... being part of a said patent
of land given to the said Charles Patty by his father's
will.
                    /s/ Charles Patty
Dated 7 September 1770   Recorded 27 Sept. 1770

Ref: Pittsylvania County Loose Papers - 1767-1770
Virginia State Library

RIVES, Thomas   Chatham County, N. C.

  Josiah Daniel and Elizabeth Daniel, his wife, of Albemarle County, State of Virginia to Thomas Rives of Mecklenburg County, State of Virginia (formerly of Amelia County) .
... cons. 230 pounds ... 400 acres on both sides of Nutbush
Creek ... adjoining the county line between Virginia and
North Carolina ... and lines of Thomas Carter and Miles
Johnson ... being 400 acres granted to John Robinson by patent in 1750, and granted to Josiah Daniel by deed recorded
in Lunenburg County.
Dated 11 January 1773   Recorded 11 Jan. 1773

 Ref: Mecklenburg County Deed Book 3, page 522

12 July 1750 - JOHN ROBINSON, 400 acres on Nutbush Creek and
     on the county line.

 Ref: Patent Book 29, page 238 - Va. State Library

M.B. 28 August 1764 - Thomas Rives and Eleanor Neal
     Surety: David Neal

 Ref: Amelia County Marriage Records, page R-1

Note: Thomas Rives married (2) Mary, but there is no known
 extant marriage record. Thomas and Eleanor (Neal)
 Rives had two children: William Rives and Joana Rives
 who were left bequests in the will of their grandfather
 David Neal of Amelia County.

 Thomas Rives gave bond and qualified as guardian for
Joana Rives and William Rives 13 October 1777.

 Ref: Mecklenburg County Guardian Book - unpaged

  A division of the estate in the hands of Thomas Rives
belonging to William and Joana Rives was made by John Kendrick and Parmenas Williams.
Dated 19 December 1786   Recorded 11 June 1787

 Ref: Mecklenburg County Will Book 2, page 210

M.B. 19 Dec. 1785 - Terisha Turner and Joanah Rives
     Surety: John Burton
  Consent: Stephen Turner for Terisha Turner
  Consent: Thomas Rives for Joanah Rives
  Married 22 December 1785 by the Rev. John King

M.B. 1 January 1788 - William Rives and Mary Turner
     Surety: Nicholas Bilbo
  Consent: Thomas Rives father of William Rives
  Consent: Stephen Turner father of Mary Turner

Ref: ELLIOTT: Mecklenburg County Marriage Records,
1765-1810, pages 105 and 124

Note: Thomas Rives sold his land in Mecklenburg County in
1796 and removed to Chatham County, North Carolina. The
Mecklenburg County Personal Property Tax Lists show
Thomas Rives with sons Edward, Robert and John Rives who
were children of his (2) marriage.

Thomas Rives of Mecklenburg County to William Hendrick
of Mecklenburg County ... cons. 400 pounds ... 400 acres on
both sides of Nutbush Creek ... bounded by the county line.
Witnesses: George Tarry
            William Bilbo   /s/ Thomas Rives
            Geo. Richardson
Dated 12 March 1796   Recorded 11 April 1796

Ref: Mecklenburg County Deed Book 9, page 71

To Samuel Hopkins and Mark Alexander, Gents:

Whereas Thomas Rives conveyed 400 acres of land to
William Hendrick, and as Mary Rives, wife of Thomas Rives,
cannot conveniently travel to this Court, you are requested
to get her release of her dower right in this land.

Court Order 30 August 1796   /s/ W. Baskervill Clk.

In obedience to order of Court, we privily examined
Mary Rives, wife of Thomas Rives, 15 October 1796, and she
voluntarily relinquished her dower.
                                     /s/ Sam Hopkins, Junr.
Recorded 14 November 1796   M. Alexander

Ref: Mecklenburg County Deed Book 9, page 160

ROBERTSON, Robert W.   Limestone County, Ala.

Know all men by these presents that I, Robert W. Robert
son of the County of Limestone, State of Alabama, have made,
nominated and appointed Benjamin O. Wilburn of the said
County of Limestone, State of Alabama, my true and lawful
attorney, for me and in my name, to demand, sue for, recover
and receive of Sally Robinson of the County of Sussex, State
of Virginia, all sums of money due me from my father's estate (name of father not given).
Dated 13 November 1826   Recorded 5 April 1827

Ref: Sussex County Deed Book "P", page 83

ROBERSON, James, et als   Giles County, Tenn.

    Know all men by these presents that I, James Roberson
of the County of Giles, State of Tennessee, but at present
in Brunswick County, State of Virginia, for and in behalf of
myself and wife Patsy, formerly Finch, in behalf of Thomas
Betty who intermarried with Rebekah Finch, and in behalf of
Mary Ann Finch, daughters and legatees of William Finch,
deceased, late of Brunswick County, State of Virginia, do by
these presents nominate and appoint Randolph Price of Brunswick County, State of Virginia, my agent, or attorney, for
me and in my name, and for and in the name of Thomas Betty
and Mary Ann Finch, to collect from,(and secure all sums due
us) the executors or administrators of the estate of William
Finch, deceased.
Dated 6 April 1813   Recorded 25 Oct. 1813

    Ref: <u>Brunswick County Deed Book 22, page 193</u>

M.B. 31 Dec. 1804 - Thomas Betty and Rebecca Finch
               Surety: David Walter (Walker ?)

M.B. 23 May 1796 - Arthur Fort and Polly Finch, daughter
               of William and Tabitha Finch
               Surety: Edwin Fort
Married 9 June 1796 by the Rev. Aaron Brown

    Ref: <u>Brunswick County Marriage Records, pages 91,149</u>

ROBERTS, John   Franklin County, Mo.

    John Roberts and Susanna Roberts, his wife, of Franklin
County, State of Missouri to Moses A. Dupree of Charlotte
County, State of Virginia .... cons. $655.25 .... tract of
land containing 272 acres .... on the waters of Horsepen and
Blueston Creeks in Charlotte County.
Dated 19 February 1833   Recorded 1 April 1833

    Ref: <u>Charlotte County Deed Book 20, page 151</u>

ROBERTS, Thomas   Barren County Ky.

    Know all men by these presents that I, Thomas Roberts
of Barren County, State of Kentucky, have by these presents
appointed John W. Allen of Barren County, State of Kentucky,
my attorney to receive of Joseph B. Clausel, administrator
of Thomas Malone, deceased, who was administrator of Isham
Malone, deceased, sums of money due to me.
Dated 8 September 1838   Recorded 15 Oct. 1838

    Ref: <u>Mecklenburg County Deed Book 28, page 48</u>

ROBERTS, Bartholomew *   Morgan County, Ga.

John Roberts and Susanna, his wife, James M. McCargo
and Prudence, his wife, all of Charlotte County, State of
Virginia, William Hatchett and Jane, his wife, of Clark
County, State of Georgia, and Bartholomew Roberts and
Rebecca, his wife, of Morgan County, State of Georgia, to
Thomas Roberts, Charlotte County, State of Virginia ....
cons. $493.33 .... 140 acres ... being the certain lots or
parcels of land that fell to them by the death of Martha
Roberts (late of Charlotte County), and which fell to her as
her dower right as the widow of Francis Roberts, deceased.
Dated 6 January 1819   Recorded 1 Feb. 1819

Ref: Charlotte County Deed Book 15, page 43

* Bartholomew Roberts is listed in Charlotte County records
  both as Bartholomew and as Bartlett Roberts.

On the motion of Martha Roberts, widow and relict of
Francis Roberts, deceased, who made oath according to law,
certificate is granted her for obtaining letters of administration of the said estate conditioned on her giving security,
Whereon she, with Thomas Chaffin, Thomas Hatchett, John
Hatchett and Archibald Hatchett her securities, entered into
and acknowledged bond according to law for that purpose.
April Court 1789

Ref: Charlotte County Order Book 7, page 246

Ordered that Matthew Burt, the Rev. John Williams,
Thomas Chaffin and William Thweatt, or any three of them,
being first sworn for that purpose, do appraise in current
money the slaves and personal property of the estate of
Francis Roberts, deceased, and make their report to the
next court.   April Court 1789

Ref: Charlotte County Order Book 7, page 246

CHANCERY SUIT

John Roberts in his own right, Prudence Roberts,
Francis Roberts, Bartholomew Roberts and Thomas Roberts, by
their guardian John Roberts, Plaintiffs
                          VS
                        Martha Roberts, widow and
the administratrix of Francis Roberts, deceased, and William
Hatchett and Jane his wife, Defendants
Pursuant to a former decreetal order made in this cause
the person^s therein named made their report in these words,
"In obedience to an order of Court to us directed, we have
proceeded to divide the estate of Francis Roberts, deceased,

between Martha Roberts, widow and relict of the said deceased, and the orphans in the following manner, Viz:
To Martha Roberts 224 acres of land, etc.
To William and Jeane (Jane) Hatchett 74 acres of land, etc.
To John Roberts 74 acres of land, etc.
To Francis Roberts 74 acres of land, etc.
To Prudence Roberts 74 acres of land, etc.
To Bartlett Roberts 74 acres of land, etc.
To Thomas Roberts 74 acres of land, etc."

/s/ Mack Goode
William Thweatt
Recorded at August Court 1791   Robert Bedford

Ref: Charlotte County Order Book 8, page 161

William Read of Charlotte County to Francis Roberts of Amelia County ... cons. 100 pounds ... 655 acres of land on both sides of Williams Fork of Horsepen Creek ... adjoining Bullard, Williams and Daniel Jones ... being land patented by Robert Williams ... and sold to William Read.
Dated 2 April 1770   Recorded 2 April 1770

Ref: Charlotte County Deed Book 2, page 274

WILL OF THOMAS ROBERTS

NAMES: Wife - Hannah Roberts
To son - John Roberts (eldest son) 200 acres, etc.
To son - Alexander Roberts 200 acres, etc.
To son - Thomas Roberts 200 acres, etc.
To son - Francis Roberts 200 acres, it being the land where I now live.
Children all minors, property to go to sons at age 21 Remainder of estate to wife Hannah Roberts during her widowhood, but if she remarries, then I desire that my estate (given her) to be divided between my five children - Alexander Roberts, Jane Roberts, Mary Roberts, Thomas Roberts and Francis Roberts.
Executor: Wife Hannah Roberts sole executor
Witnesses: George Booker, John Burton, Edward Booker, Jr.
Dated 9 Sept. 1734   Recorded 12 August 1737

Ref: Amelia County Will Book 1, page 5

Francis, son of Thomas and Hannah Roberts, born 29 June 1733

Ref: Bristol Parish Register, page 360

Francis Roberts of Amelia County to Daniel Wilson of Amelia County ... cons. 200 pounds ... 200 acres .... part of land which was granted to Thomas Roberts by patent .....

adjoining Daniel Wilson et als.
Dated 15 July 1754   Recorded 26 Sept. 1754

    Ref: Amelia County Deed Book 5, page 192

    Francis Roberts and Martha, his wife, of Raleigh Parish
Amelia County, to Joel Jackson of the same Parish and County
... cons. 225 pounds ... 250 acres ... being land granted to
James Long 10 Sept. 1735 ... and now by several conveyances
vested in Francis Roberts.
Dated 8 April 1765   Recorded 23 May 1765

    Ref: Amelia County Deed Book 8, page 546

M.B. 3 Dec. 1787 - William Hatchett and Jane Roberts, dau.
                   of Francis Roberts
                   Surety: John Roberts

M.B. 21 Jan. 1788 - John Roberts and Susanna Pettus *
                    Surety: William Hatchett

M.B. 6 Oct. 1797 - Francis Roberts and Jane Herndon, dau. of
                   Joseph Herndon
                   Surety: John Roberts

M.B. 8 May 1798 - James McCargo and Prudence Roberts, dau.
                  of Martha Roberts
                  Surety: John Roberts

M.B. 26 Dec. 1800 - Bartlett Roberts and Rebecca M. Fears
                    Married by the Rev. Edward Almond

M.B. 7 March 1803 - Thomas Roberts and Sallie Herndon, dau.
                    of Joseph Herndon
                    Surety: Francis Roberts
         Married 10 March 1803 by the Rev. Edward Almond

* This marriage record is in Lunenburg County - the others
  in Charlotte County.

    John Brooke and Sarah, his wife, and Francis Roberts
and Martha, his wife, all of Charlotte County, to Stephen
Neal of Amelia County ... cons. 25000 pounds of neat in-
spected tobacco ... 250 acres in Amelia County ...on the
south fork of Horsepen Branch ... adjoining the lands of
Branch Tanner, Abraham Marshall, Joseph Osborne and Stephen
Neal.
Dated 27 October 1785   Recorded 28 Oct. 1785

    Ref: Amelia County Deed Book 17, page 282

ROBERTS, Jesse   Rutherford County, Tenn.

Know all men by these presents that I, Jesse Roberts of
Rutherford County, State of Tennessee, have made, ordained,
constituted and appointed George Clanton of the County of
Henry, State of Virginia, my attorney, in my name, to sell
and convey all of my right, title, claim and interest there-
to, according to the Laws of Virginia, in and to a certain
tract of land lying and being in the County of Henry, State
of Virginia (acreage and location not stated).
Dated 24 March 1818   Recorded June Court 1818

Ref: Henry County Deed Book 8, page 262

SHELL, Byron   Hancock County, Ga.

Know all men by these presents that I, Byron Shell of
Hancock County, State of Georgia, for divers good causes and
considerations, have made, authorized, nominated and appointed David Thomas of the County of Hancock, State of Georgia,
my true and lawful attorney, for me and in my name and for
my use, to sell a certain tract of land in the County of
Brunswick, State of Virginia, containing 133 acres which
said land was given to me by my father Stephen Shell of the
County of Brunswick, and my attorney is to act as fully as
if I were present in person.
Dated 12 September 1805   Recorded 28 Oct. 1805

Ref: Brunswick County Deed Book 19, page 339

SHELL, William   State of S. C.

To all whom it may concern, Know ye that I, William
Shell, Senr., of the County of Brunswick, State of Virginia,
for divers good causes and considerations, being about to
remove to South Carolina, have made, constituted and appointed, in my place and stead, my son Lemon Shell of the County of Brunswick, State of Virginia, my true and lawful attorney, for me and in my name and for my use, to sell all of
my lands lying in the County of Brunswick, and to transact
all of my business in the State of Virginia.
Dated 29 October 1797   Recorded 25 June 1798

Ref: Brunswick County Deed Book 17, page 255

M.B. 24 Nov. 1795 - Jesse Beshears and Betsy Shell, age 21
                 Surety: William Shell

Ref: Brunswick County Marriage Records, page 88

SIMMONS, Benjamin et als   Hancock County, Ga.

     Know all men by these presents that we, Benjamin
Simmons in the right of my wife Sally Simmons of the County
of Hancock, State of Georgia, George Stovall of the County
of Putnam, State of Georgia, Joseph Stovall of the County of
Baldwin, State of Georgia, John Hunt in the right of my wife
Ruth Hunt of the County of Jasper, State of Georgia, and
Pleasant Stovall of the County of Richmond, State of Georgia
all of the aforesaid being heirs of Thomas Stovall, deceased
late of the County of Henry, State of Virginia, do hereby
nominate, constitute and appoint Joseph Stovall and George
Penn of the County of Patrick, State of Virginia, our true
and lawful attorneys, for us and in our names, to sell and
convey a certain tract of land on Marrowbone Creek in the
County of Henry, State of Virginia, it being the tract of
land whereon Thomas Stovall lived previous to his death, and
we ratify and confirm whatsoever our attorneys do in our
names.
Dated 2 August 1814   Recorded 13 Feb. 1815

     Ref: Henry County Deed Book 8, page 43

     Thomas Stovall died intestate. Inventory and appraisal
of the estate of Thomas Stovall, deceased, made by William
Moody, James Taylor and Daniel Taylor - valuation 457 pounds
5 shillings 11 pence - returned to Court by Joseph Stovall,
administrator, and Elizabeth Stovall, widow and relict, administratrix.   No date of recording

     Ref: Henry County Will Book 1, page 226

     An account current of the estate of Thomas Stovall,
deceased - 1793-1805 - returned to Court and ordered to be
recorded.   Recorded Sept. Court 1805

     Ref: Henry County Will Book 2, page 258

     Receipts for their proportionate part of the estate of
Thomas Stovall, deceased, presented in Court by the administrator, and ordered to be recorded.
1. Receipt from Joseph Cooper for Joseph Stovall, Polly
   Stovall and Pleasant Stovall.
2. Receipt from George Stovall.
3. Receipt from Benjamin Simmons.
4. Receipt from John Weeks as guardian for Ruth Stovall.
5. Receipt from John Weeks who married the widow and administratrix of Thomas Stovall.   Rec. 18 March 1807

     Ref: Henry County Will Book 2, page 194

SIMS, Frederick   Wilkes County, Ga.

      To all whom these presents come, Know ye that I,
Frederick Sims of Wilkes County, State of Georgia, have by
these presents constituted and appointed Drury Stith of the
County of Brunswick, State of Virginia, my attorney for me
and in my name to sell and convey a certain tract of land
situate, lying and being in Brunswick County on the Meherrin
River, containing 543 acres more or less, to William Edward
Broadnax, and my attorney shall do all lawful acts as if I
were present in person.
Dated 14 March 1788   Recorded 13 Aug. 1788

      Ref: Brunswick County Deed Book 14, page 465

Note: Recorded in Wilkes County, Georgia, Deed Book "DD" at
      page 32.

TARWATER, George T.   Hempstead County, Ark.

      Know all men by these presents that we, Thomas Owen and
Frances Owen (wife of the said Thomas Owen), Quincy E. Ligon
and Phebe Ligon, all of Mecklenburg County, State of Virginia, have appointed George T. Tarwater of the County of
Hempstead, State of Arkansas, our lawful attorney to take
possession of and sell certain slaves due us ... being the
property willed to us by our grandfather John Stovall, deceased, late of Granville County, State of North Carolina,
and conveyed in trust by our father, the late Obadiah Ligon,
deceased, of Mecklenburg County ... the said slaves being
carried to Hempstead County, State of Arkansas, by William
B. Easley formerly of Mecklenburg County.
Dated 21 August 1843   Recorded 31 Aug. 1843

      Ref: Mecklenburg County Deed Book 30, page 522

SPEED, Joseph   Tioga County, N. Y.

      Joseph Speed of the County of Tioga, State of New York,
to John Speed of the County of Mecklenburg, State of Virginia ... cons. $2,700.00 paid to him in the County of Tioga,
State of New York ...has by these presents sold to the said
John Speed all of his right and interest in that part of his
father's estate, both real and personal, which was willed to
the use of our mother Sarah Speed ... as can be shown by the
last will and testament of our said father ... together with
the future increase of slaves. (Joseph Speed personally appeared before the Court to acknowledge this bill of sale)
Dated 22 Feb. 1821   Recorded 7 March 1825

      Ref: Mecklenburg County Deed Book 19, page 13

SPAIN, Susanna   Mecklenburg County, N. C.

     Know all men by these presents that we, Susanna Spain,
late Susanna McKinne(y), Elizabeth McKinne(y) and Fanny
McKinne(y) of Mecklenburg County, State of North Carolina,
do by these presents appoint out trusty friend Thomas Proctor of Wake County, State of North Carolina, our attorney to
sell a tract of land in Brunswick County, State of Virginia,
containing 100 acres which was conveyed to us by Buckner
Stith of the State of Virginia ... the said land was conveyed to Susanna McKinne(y), now Spain, during her lifetime and
at her death to the said Elizabeth McKinne(y) and Fanny
McKinne(y) forever.
     And our attorney is to sell and convey the said land
for and for our use as if we were present in person.
Dated 26 January 1805   Recorded 28 April 1806

     Ref: Brunswick County Deed Book 19, page 438

SMITH, Samuel Henry   Marengo County, Ala.

     Know all men by these presents that I, Samuel Henry
Smith of Marengo County, State of Alabama, do by these presents appoint my brothers John P. Smith and James Smith of
Granville County, State of North Carolina, my attorneys
(both or either to act) to execute a deed and act for me and
in my name as one of the executors of my father James Smith,
deceased, of Granville County, State of North Carolina, and
particularly to sign a deed for four lots in the town of
Clarksville on the Roanoke River in Mecklenburg County, which
said lots have been sold but my name is necessary as one of
the executors.
Dated 13 July 1833   Recorded 15 Sept. 1834

     Ref: Mecklenburg County Deed Book 26, page 148

SMITH, William F.   Lincoln County, Tenn.

     Know all men by these presents that I, William F. Smith
of Lincoln County, State of Tennessee, have appointed my
brother John P. Smith of Granville County, State of North
Carolina, my legal attorney, for me and in my name, to sell
and convey all of my interest in and to four lots in the
town of Clarksville, Mecklenburg County, State of Virginia.
Dated 18 July 1833   Recorded 15 Sept. 1834

     Ref: Mecklenburg County Deed Book 26, page 148

STARLING, William, et als   Mercer County, Ky.

Know all men by these presents that I, Henry Lyne of
Henry County, State of Virginia, one of the heirs and legatees of Edmund Lyne, deceased, of Bourbon County, State of
Kentucky, do appoint my trusty friend William Starling of
Mercer County, State of Kentucky, my true and lawful attorney in my name, as a legatee of the aforesaid Edmund Lyne,
deceased, to convey in fee simple a tract of land, being in
the Northwest Territory on the Ohio River near the mouth of
Eagle Creek, containing by estimation 1000 acres, to Alexander Dorr of the County of Mason, State of Kentucky, and to
receive from him the consideration paid for the same.
Dated 24 December 1800   Recorded 29 Dec. 1800

     Ref: Henry County Deed Book 6, page 259

WEAKLEY, Robert   Robertson County, Tenn.

Know all men by these presents that I, Robert Weakley
of Robertson County, State of Tennessee (husband to Jane
Weakley a legatee of Robert Weakley, deceased, late of Halifax County, State of Virginia, do by these presents relinguish all of my right, title, interest and demand in and to
a certain tract of land, containing by estimation 77 acres
... in Halifax County adjoining the land of Thomas Bush,
Fleman Hoggis, William Tucker and John Hoggis ... which
tract of land was left by the last will and testament of the
aforesaid Robert Weakley, deceased, to my wife for life and
then to descend to her heirs. I do relinquish the said
right and title to Robert Fambrough, and in the future lay
no claims or demands on this tract of land.
Dated 20 September 1801   Recorded 26 July 1802

     Ref: Halifax County Deed Book 19, page 322

M.B. 25 March 1793 - Robert Weakley and Jane Fambrough
                 Surety: Samuel Weakley

M.B. 23 Sept. 1793 - Robert Fambrough and Mary Gunston
                 Surety: Samuel Weakley

     Ref: Halifax County Marriage Records, pages 27, 28

M.B. 2 October 1795 - William Steel and Polly Fambrough
                 Surety: Robert Weakley
       Married 4 Oct. 1795 by the Rev. Hawkins Landrum

     Ref: Halifax County Marriage Records, page 32

TAYLOR, Drury   Rutherford County, N. C.

Drury Taylor of the County of Rutherford, State of
North Carolina, to Daniel Jones of Halifax County, State of
Virginia ... cons. 100 pounds ... all right, title and int-
erest of Drury Taylor and Sarah Taylor, his wife, in and to
a tract of land on the north side of the Dan River on Miry
Creek (in Halifax County) containing 100 acres more or less,
being the undivided interest in land left by John Jones,
Senr., to David Jones and John Jones (Job Jones ?).
Dated 15 October 1800   Recorded 24 Feb. 1801

Ref: Halifax County Deed Book 18, page 543

WILL OF JOB JONES

NAMES: Wife - Sarah Jones
       Mentions children but not by name.
       Entire estate left to wife Sarah Jones.
       Land to be sold by wife Sarah Jones at her desire.
Executors: Wife Sarah Jones and Charles Mullins
Dated 15 June 1786   Recorded 5 March 1787

Ref: Halifax County Will Book 2, page 199

Note: There is no extant marriage record but Drury Taylor
      married Sarah Jones, widow of Job Jones.

WILL OF JOHN JONES

NAMES: Wife - Jane Jones
       Son - Eldest son David Jones
       Daughters - Susanna Jones, Margaret Jones
       Son - Youngest son Job Jones
       Brother-in-law William Douglas
Executors: Wife Jane Jones and brother-in-law William
           Douglas
Dated 5 October 1772   Recorded 18 Nov. 1773

Ref: Halifax County Will Book 1, page 48

TURNER, William   Anson County, S. C.

William Turner of Anson County, State of North Carolina
to John Turner of Cumberland County, State of Virginia ....
cons. 105 pounds ... 190 acres on Branches of Mountain Creek
... Mecklenburg County, State of Virginia ... adjoining the
lines of Clack and McDaniel.
Dated 1 October 1791   Recorded 11 Feb. 1793

Ref: Mecklenburg County Deed Book 8, page 264

TAYLOR, William   Autauga County, Ala.

    Know all men by these presents that we, William Taylor
and Nancy Taylor, his wife, do by these presents appoint
Samuel Pannill of the County of Campbell, State of Virginia,
our attorney in fact to transact such business as may be
necessary in settlement of the estate of John Collins, deceased, of Halifax County, State of Virginia, and to collect
any money coming to us.
Dated 10 April 1840   Recorded 25 May 1840

        Ref: Halifax County Deed Book 46, page 276

M.B. 21 July 1792 - William Taylor and Nancy Collins
                    Surety: James Collins

        Ref: Halifax County Marriage Records, page 23

    RECEIPT: I, Samuel Pannill of Green Hill, Campbell
County, State of Virginia, acting attorney for William Taylor and wife Nancy, daughter of the late John Collins, have
this day received of William Collins, executor of the said
John Collins, deceased, the sum of $649.20½ being the whole
amount received by me for the said William and Nancy Taylor.
Dated 20 May 1840   Recorded 25 May 1840

        Ref: Halifax County Deed Book 46, page 276

COLLINS, Peter et als   Henderson County, Tenn.

    Know all men by these presents that we, James Collins
of Halifax County, State of Virginia, Peter Collins in his
own right and under a power of attorney for Joseph Collins,
Elisha Collins and Sally Hix of Henderson County, State of
Tennessee, Tyree Carter in his own right and under a power
of attorney for John Collins, Junr., of Hart County, State
of Kentucky, and William Collins of Halifax County, State of
Virginia, now
    Whereas a certain John Collins, deceased, died in poss-
ession and title of 351 acres of land on Buffalo Creek, a
part of which is in Pittsylvania County, and also a tract of
188 acres in Halifax County on the drafts of Runaway Creek
... which land was devised by will of the said John Collins,
deceased, to be sold and proceeds divided among his children, now
    We do by these presents agree that the said tracts of
land are to be sold by William Collins, executor of the
estate of John Collins, deceased, as provided by the will,
at public auction to the high bidder.
Dated 23 August 1838   Recorded 23 Aug. 1838

        Ref: Halifax County Deed Book 46, page 278

TORIAN, Jacob   Christian County, Ky.

        Know all men by these presents that I, Jacob Torian of
Christian County, State of Kentucky, do constitute and appoint Dr. James Mudd and Thomas Torian of Halifax County,
State of Virginia, my attornies in fact, and in my stead, to
sell that tract of land ... in right of my wife Polly Torian
which descended by death of her father, Robertson Owen, of
Halifax County, State of Virginia ... and to collect any
sums due me from Robertson Owen, Junr., administrator of the
said Robertson Owen, Senr., deceased.
Dated 13 Sept. 1819   Recorded 23 Oct. 1820

        Ref: Halifax County Deed Book 29, page 10

M.B. 13 June 1803 - Jacob Torian and Polly Owen
                    Surety: John Owen
             Robertson Owen father of Polly Owen
        Ref: Halifax County Marriage Records

        Peter Torian, Senr., George Torian and Martha, his
wife, and Jacob Torian and Mary, his wife, of Halifax County, to Thomas Torian of Halifax County ... cons. 849 pounds
9 shillings and other good causes, them hereunto moving, do
grant, bargain and sell to the said Thomas Torian ... 404½
acres on the north side of the Dan River adjoining Scare
Torian.
Dated 25 Sept. 1810   Recorded 22 Oct. 1810
        Ref: Halifax County Deed Book 22, page 522

                        CHANCERY SUIT

        William Owen, Thomas E. Owen, Jacob Torian and Polly,
his wife, Nancy Owen, Polly Owen, Robert Owen and Thomas
Owen, children of John Owen, deceased, who being infants sue
by their next friend Thomas Easley, Obedience Torian and
Nancy Torian, infant children of Nancy Torian, deceased,
formerly Nancy Owen, who sue by their next friend and father
Scare Torian, Junr., Plaintiffs
                        VS
                        Robertson Owen and Margaret
Owen, Defendants,
                Ordered that James Bruce, John Ragland,
Senr., William Bailey, Samuel Williams and Nathaniel Terry,
or any three of them, divide the lands of Robertson Owen,
Senr., deceased.   Recorded at Feb. Court 1819
        Ref: Halifax County Plea Book 35, page 49

M.B. 16 Dec. 1802 - Scare Torian and Nancy R. Owen

        Ref: Halifax County Marriage Records, page 50

                            111

THWEATT, Drury   Jasper County, Ga.

Know all men by these presents that I, Drury Thweatt of
Jasper County, State of Georgia, for divers good causes and
considerations, me hereunto moving, have made, ordained,
constituted and appointed Vines Harwell of the County of
Morgan, State of Georgia, my true and lawful attorney, for
me and in my name and for my use, to ask, demand, recover
and receive of and from the administrator or executor of the
late William Thweatt, deceased, as one of his heirs or distributees of the said William Thweatt, all property which
may have been willed or left to me.
Dated 6 March 1823   Recorded April Court 1823

Ref: Brunswick County Deed Book 25, page 509

TUCKER, Mary Ann   Hancock County, Ga.

Know all men by these presents that I, Mary Ann Tucker
of Hancock County, State of Georgia, for divers good causes
and considerations, me hereunto moving, have made, ordained
and appointed my nephew Benjamin I. Harper of the County of
Hancock, State of Georgia, for me and in my name and for my
use, to sell and convey all of my real and personal estate
in the County of Brunswick, State of Virginia, and to do all
lawful acts as fully as if I were present.
Dated 9 May 1821   Recorded Oct. Court 1821

Ref: Brunswick County Deed Book 25, page 215

M.B. 22 Nov. 1790 - Thomas Ingram and Mary Ann Ingram
                    Surety: Charles Harris

M.B. 7 Jan. 1804 - Sterling Tucker and Mary Ann Ingram
                   Surety: Hartwell Tucker
          Married 12 Jan. 1804 by the Rev. Wright Tucker

Ref: Brunswick County Marriage Records, pp. 61, 145

Note: No will of Thomas Ingram has been found in Brunswick
      County records, but the will of Sterling Tucker leaves
      his estate to wife Mary Ann Tucker and his brother
      Hartwell Tucker. The will refers to property left
      Mary Ann Tucker, his wife, by her (1) husband Thomas
      Ingram.

M.B. 25 Aug. 1800 - Benjamin Harper and Nancy Ingram, dau.
                    of John Ingram
                    Surety: Thomas Ingram

Ref: Brunswick County Marriage records, page 122

VINCENT, Thomas, et als   Lancaster District, S. C.

        Know all men by these presents that we, Thomas Vincent
and Rebekah Vincent, children and heirs of Peter Vincent,
late of Lancaster District, State of South Carolina, for
divers good causes and considerations, do make, ordain,
authorize, nominate and appoint Henry Vincent of Lancaster
District, State of South Carolina, our true and lawful attorney to ask, demand, sue for, recover and receive of and
from Joshua Vincent of the County of Northampton, State of
North Carolina, agent for the estate of Peter Vincent, formerly of the County of Greensville, State of Virginia, deceased, all sums of money, debts and legacies which may be
due to us, the said Thomas and Rebekah Vincent, from the
said Joshua Vincent, Agent.
Dated 12 December 1805

        I assign the within power of attorney to John Robinson
and William Fox of Greensville County, State of Virginia, to
act on as if I were present in person.
                                    /s/ Joshua Vincent
                                Recorded Feb. Court 1806

        Ref: Greensville County Deed Book 3, page 342

        Inventory and appraisal of the estate of Peter Vincent,
deceased, made by Foster Cook, Henry Wyche, Junr., and John
Robinson made 3 December 1805, returned to Court and ordered
to be recorded.
                                    December Court 1805

        Ref: Greensville County Will Book 1, page 550

Note: Peter Vincent died intestate, evidently, as no will is
      recorded in Greensville County.

VINCENT, Ann   Lancaster District, S. C.

        Know all men by these presents that I, Ann Vincent of
Lancaster District, State of South Carolina, for divers good
causes, me hereunto moving, have made, ordained, authorized,
nominated and appointed Henry Vincent of Lancaster District,
State of South Carolina, my true and lawful attorney, for me
and in my name, to ask, demand, sue for, recover and receive
of and from the agents of the estate of Thomas Powell all
such sum or sums of money which are now due and owing unto
me, the said Ann Vincent, by and from the agents of Thomas
Powell, deceased, and to act for me in every way as if I
were present in person.
Dated 4 September 1805   Recorded Jan. Court 1806

        Ref: Greensville County Deed Book 3, page 449

WILL OF THOMAS POWELL

NAMES: Wife - Sarah Powell
      Daughters - Sylvia Collier, Ann Vincent
      Son - William Powell
      Grandson - Dixon Cato
      Grandchildren - Sally Cato, Robert Cato, Wiley Cato,
                Rolling Cato, William Cato.
Executors: Son William Powell and wife Sara Powell
Dated 5 September 1794   Recorded Feb. Court 1796

    Ref: Greensville County Will Book 1, page 318

CHRISMAN, William   Knox County, Indiana Terr.

    Know all men by these presents that I, William Chrisman
of the County of Knox, Indiana Territory, in the right of my
wife Polly, who was Polly Taylor daughter and representative
of Benjamin Taylor, deceased, late of Lunenburg County,
State of Virginia, for divers good causes and considerations
me hereunto moving, have by these presents nominated, constituted and appointed my trusty friend Robert M. Evans of the
said County of Knox and Territory of Indiana, my true and
lawful attorney, for me and in my name, to ask, demand and
receive of the administrators or executors of the said Benjamin Taylor, deceased, all of the estate both real and personal which may be coming to my wife, and my attorney is to
do whatsoever I myself could do if I were present in person.
Dated 3 September 1811   Recorded 11 Oct. 1811

    Ref: Lunenburg County Deed Book 22, page 155

    Inventory and appraisal of the estate of Benjamin Tay-
lor, deceased, taken 3 August 1810 by Thomas Adams, Wilfred
Maddox and Phillip Burnett - valuation 4448 pounds, 2 shillings 9 pence - returned to Court 13 September 1810 and ordered to be recorded.

    Ref: Lunenburg County Will Book 7, page 8

LYNCH, John   Surry County, N. C.

    John Lynch of Surry County, State of North Carolina to
Benjamin Pulliam of Mecklenburg County, State of Virginia ..
cons. 60 pounds ... 150 acres ... adjoining Lidderdale,
Wilson and Brame.
Dated 4 March 1778   Recorded 8 March 1779

    Ref: Mecklenburg County Deed Book 5, page 397

WORTHAM, Thomas P.   Maury County, Tenn.

    Know all men by these presents that I, Thomas P.
Wortham of the County of Maury, State of Tennessee, by these
presents have appointed William Hendrick of Mecklenburg
County, State of Virginia, my lawful attorney in my name as
guardian of Stephen P. H. Wright to receive from John M.
Wright of Mecklenburg County, State of Virginia, the former
guardian of Stephen P. H. Wright, the sum of sixteen dollars
sixty six and two-third cents due to the said Stephen from
Unity C. Wright in a division of slaves, and to receive from
John M. Wright certain negroes and to transport them to
Tennessee for me.
Dated 6 October 1837   Recorded 18 Feb. 1839

    Ref: Mecklenburg County Deed Book 28, page 156

M.B. 17 Dec. 1823 - Thomas P. Wortham and Eliza H. Davis
                Surety: Horace Palmer
        Consent: William Hendrick guardian of Eliza H. Davis

M.B. 10 March 1838 - John M. Wright and Jane Davis
                Surety: James T. Russell
        Consent: John Davis father of Jane Davis

M.B. 18 April 1814 - Reuben Wright and Unity C. Davis
                Surety: Green Blanton

        Ref: Mecklenburg County Marriage Records, 1811-1853
                        Pages 191, 192, 193

RICHARDSON, Conrad   Williamson County, Tenn.

    Know all men by these presents that I, Conrad Richard-
son of Williamson County, State of Tennessee, do appoint my
friend Josiah Johnson of Williamson County, State of Tennessee, my true and lawful attorney to make a deed to John Wood
of Williamson County, State of Tennessee, for a tract of
land containing 85 acres in Charlotte County, State of Virginia, on the head waters of Meherrin Creek ... adjoining the
land of my wife Elizabeth Richardson (late Elizabeth Fuqua)
... being land deeded to me by Doctor Fuqua.
Dated 24 March 1813   Recorded 3 May 1813

    Ref: Charlotte County Deed Book 12, page 179

M.B. 21 July 1789 - Josiah Johnson and Susanna Martin
                Surety: Abraham Martin
        Married 24 July 1789 by the Rev. Thomas Johnston

    Ref: Charlotte County Marriage Records, page 137

Matthew Walker and Sally Walker, his wife, of Greene
County, State of Georgia, to George Rogers of Mecklenburg
County, State of Virginia ... cons. $1,100.00 ... 550 acres
on both sides of St. Tammany Road.
Dated 23 December 1828   Recorded 19 Jan. 1829

Ref: Mecklenburg County Deed Book 23, page 368

M.B. 4 Oct. 1809 - Matthew Walker and Sally Stone
                    Surety: William Stone
      Married 19 Oct. 1809 by the Rev. Richard Dabbs

Note: Matthew Walker son of Aurelius and Nancy (Turner)
      Walker
      Sally Stone daughter of William and Hannah (Love)
      Stone

M.B. 23 Nov. 1784 - Aurelius Walker and Nancy Turner
                    Surety: William Allen

Note: Aurelius Walker son of Sylvanus Walker and his (1)
      wife (unknown)
      Nancy Turner daughter of Matthew Turner

WILL OF MATTHEW TURNER

EXCERPT:
        To Aurelius Walker and my daughter Nancy (Walker)
... during their natural lives ... 250 acres of land on Cox
Creek, where they now live ... five negroes ... at their
death to go to their children, etc.
Dated 23 Feb. 1800   Recorded 14 April 1800

Ref: Mecklenburg County Will Book 4, page 188

Ref: ELLIOTT: Mecklenburg County Marriage Records,
            1765-1810, pages 127-128

Note: There are no known extant marriage records for
      Sylvanus Walker, but he is said to have married (1)
      a Wade name unknown but not proven. The will of
      Robert Wade, Senr., recorded in Halifax County, names
      grandson Benjamin Walker.

Ref: ELLIOTT: Emigration from Southside Virginia,
            Volume I, page 48.

Sylvanus Walker is thought to have married (2) Susannah
Hightower, widow of William Hightower of Amelia County.
George Hightower Walker, named in the following will, was
apparently the only child of the (2) marriage of Sylvanus
Walker.

WILL OF SYLVANUS WALKER

NAMES: Wife - Susannah Walker
       Children - Benjamin Walker, Ann Smithson, Elizabeth
                  Rudd, Paulina Smith, Molly Andrews,
                  William Walker, Tandy Walker, Aurelius
                  Walker, George Hightower Walker.
       Specific bequests to children.
       Estate to wife Susannah Walker for life or widowhood,
       and then to son George Hightower Walker.
Executors: Wife Susannah Walker, Elisha Arnold, Samuel
           Marshall
Witnesses: Charles Kirks, Ichabod Smith, Sally Arnold
Dated 31 December 1785   Recorded 12 June 1786

Ref: Mecklenburg County Will Book 2, page 175

CHANCERY SUIT

Sylvanus Walker and Susannah Walker, his wife
                         VS
George Hightower and Joshua Hightower, executors of
the estate of William Walker, deceased.

By agreement of the parties, this suit is ordered to be
dismissed.
                                         May Court 1773

Ref: Lunenburg County Order Book 13, page 312

John Michaux of Lunenburg County to Sylvanus Walker of
Lunenburg County ... cons. 100 pounds ... 400 acres on the
north side of the Meherrin River and on both sides of
Crouches Creek ... being the land granted to Abram Michaux
by patent dated 30 August 1744.
Dated 5 November 1746   Recorded 6 July 1747

Note: The foregoing deed was certified for recording on 6th
      July 1747, but was not actually recorded until 1 April
      1755 after Sarah Michaux, wife of John Michaux, had
      released her dower right in the land.

Ref: Lunenburg County Deed Book 4, page

Sylvanus Walker of Lunenburg County to Benjamin Walker
of Lunenburg County ... cons. .. the said Sylvanus Walker
out of love and good will to his son Benjamin Walker, and
in consideration of the promise made him on his marrying
Mr. Joseph Minor's daughter ... 200 acres on the east side
of Crouches Creek.
Dated 7 July 1771   Recorded 11 July 1771

Ref: Lunenburg County Deed Book 12 page

Sylvanus Walker, Senr., and Susannah Walker, his wife, of Lunenburg County to Henry Blagrave of Lunenburg County ,,. cons. 8 pounds 9 shillings 6 pence current money of Virginia ... 200 acres on the north side of the Meherrin River.
Dated 11 February 1773   Recorded 11 Feb. 1773

        Ref: Lunenburg County Deed Book 12, page

    Rowland Andrews of Mecklenburg County to Sylvanus Walker of Lunenburg County ... cons. 65 pounds ... 105 acres on the south side of the Meherrin River ... adjoining James Cooper ... being land granted to Rowland Andrews by patent.
Dated 14 June 1773   Recorded 14 June 1773

        Ref: Mecklenburg County Deed Book 4, page 71

Benjamin Walker, son of Sylvanus Walker, married Letitia Minor, daughter of Joseph Minor and Edith (Cox) Minor, but there is no extant marriage record known to the compiler.

        11 Oct. 1750 - Joseph Minor and Edith Cox

        Ref: Early Marriages of Lunenburg County, 1746-1761

Ann Walker, daughter of Sylvanus Walker, married John John Smithson, but there is no extant marriage bond.

    Deed of gift from Sylvanus Walker to John Smithson ordered to be recorded.
                                        Court 14 May 1772

        Ref: Lunenburg County Order Book 13, page 188

Elizabeth Walker, daughter of Sylvanus Walker, married (1) Robert Ingram, but there is no extant marriage bond.

    Deed of gift by Sylvanus Walker of a negro boy to daughter Elizabeth Ingram and son-in-law Robert Ingram.
                                        19 March 1774

        Ref: Lunenburg County Deed Book 4, page 280

M.B. 6 March 1783 - Thomas Rudd and Elizabeth Ingram
                Surety: Sylvanus Walker

        Ref: Lunenburg County Marriage Records

Paulina Walker, daughter of Sylvanus Walker, married John Smith, but there is no extant marriage bond.

        Ref. ELLIOTT: Early Wills, 1765-1799, Mecklenburg
                County, page 80

Molly (Mary) Walker, daughter of Sylvanus Walker, married
George Andrews, son of Ephraim and Anne Andrews, but there
is no extant marriage bond.

Ref: ELLIOTT: Emigration from Southside Virginia,
        Volume I, page 18

Deed of gift from Sylvanus Walker of a negro boy to
daughter Molly Andrews and son-in-law George Andrews.
                                            8 June 1778

Ref: Lunenburg County Deed Book 5, page 314

M.B. 14 December 1789 - George (Hightower)Walker and Phebe
                        Cheatham
                        Surety: Obadiah Cheatham
                        Consent: Daniel Cheatham father of
                        Phebe Cheatham

Ref: ELLIOTT: Mecklenburg County Marriage Records,
        1765-1810, page 127

Mar. Rec. 27 Sept. 1781 - William Stone and Hannah Love *

Mar. Rec. 22 Nove 1791 - William Stone and Tabitha Neal **

* Minister's return of the Rev. James Shelburne.
** Minister's return of the Rev. William Creath.

Ref: Lunenburg County Marriage Records

WILL OF WILLIAM STONE

NAMES: Wife - Tabitha Stone - William Stone being far advan-
            ced in age, leaves to wife Tabitha for her
            natural life land, slaves, furniture, etc.
       Son - Isaac Stone - land in Pittsylvania County where
            he now lives, etc.
       Son - Asher Stone - land he now lives on, etc.
       Daughter - Sally Walker - bequests.
       Daughter - Polly Jones - bequest.
       Son - Samuel Stone - bequest.
       Daughter - Hannah Wilson - bequest.
       Daughter - Susannah Roffe - bequest.
       All land not disposed of above to be sold and after
       payment of debts balance to be divided into 9 parts.
       One part to each of my 7 living children, one part
       to children of Nancy Hutcheson, one part to children
       of my son William Stone.
       Grandchildren - Bequest to grandson William A. Stone,
       bequest to granddaughter Mary Shelburne, bequests to
       children (not named) of my daughter Nancy Hutcheson.
Executors: Son Asher Stone and Robert B. Wilson

Witnesses: Daniel Stone, William Tucker, Nancy H. Stone
Dated 18 February 1828   Recorded 21 July 1828

       Ref: Mecklenburg County Will Book 11, page 388

M.B. 9 May 1808 - Robert Wilson and Hannah Stone, daughter
                  of William Stone
                  Surety: William Stone

       Ref: Mecklenburg County Marriage Records, page 134

WARREN, William   Madison County, Ky.

     William Warren of the County of Madison, State of
Kentucky, to Robert Prunty of the County of Franklin, State
of Virginia ... cons. 100 pounds ... 100 acres more or less
... adjoining Elisha Estes and John James.
Dated 12 Nov. 1803   Recorded 2 April 1804

       Ref: Franklin County Deed Book 4, page 587

     To all whom these presents come, Know ye that I Thomas
Warren of Franklin County, State of Virginia, do hereby give
and grant all of the property which I possess and the tract
of land whereon I now live, and two negroes, namely Daniel
and Grace, and all household property to my five sons,
     Namely, Zachariah Warren, Ambrose Warren, Drury Warren,
William Warren and Elijah Warren, to be equally divided between them at my decease and at the death of my wife Jane
Warren.
Dated 12 August 1801   Recorded Sept. Court 1801

       Ref: Franklin County Deed Book 4, page 184

     John Ramsey of Patrick Parish, County of Henry, State
of Virginia, to Thomas Warren of the Parish of Patrick,
County of Henry, State of Virginia ... cons. 100 pounds ...
75 acres more or less on the north fork of Chestnut Creek .
... being land granted by patent to John Ramsey 10 August
1759.
Dated 24 June 1779   Recorded 24 June 1779

       Ref: Henry County Deed Book 1, page 242

     Zachariah Warren, Drury Warren, William Warren and
Nancy Warren, legatees of Thomas Warren, deceased, late of
the County of Franklin, State of Virginia ... cons. 40
pounds ... a certain tract of land containing 100 acres more
or less ... on the north side of the north fork of Chestnut
Creek ... for the consideration stated, receipt of which is
hereby acknowledged, convey said tract to Elijah Warren of
Franklin County ... said land being a part of a tract of

land granted to John Ramsey by patent dated 10 August 1759,
Dated 3 Sept. 1810   Recorded 3 Sept. 1810

    Ref: Franklin County Deed Book 6, page 35

M.B. 27 Feb. 1787 - Elijah Warren and Sarah Mason, daughter
                    of Robert Mason
                    Surety: Thomas Warden

    Ref: Franklin County Marriage Records, page 235

    Thomas Warren of Cumberland Parish, Lunenburg County,
to George Andrews of St. James Parish, Mecklenburg County
... cons. 200 pounds ... 220 acres on Nelsons Creek ... adjoining Jesse Brown and Valentine Brown.
Dated 14 August 1777   Recorded 14 Aug. 1777

    Ref: Lunenburg County Deed Book 13, page 39

    Jesse Brown of Cumberland Parish, Lunenburg County, to
Thomas Warren of Cumberland Parish, Lunenburg County ....
cons. 70 pounds ... 200 acres on Nelsons Creek ... adjoining
Jesse Brown and Valentine Brown.
Dated 7 Sept. 1756   Recorded 7 Dec. 1756

    Ref: Lunenburg County Deed Book 4, page 352

    Valentine Brown of Cumberland Parish, Lunenburg County,
to Thomas Warren of the said county and Parish ... cons. 5
shillings ... 20 acres on the southside of Warrens Creek.
Dated 12 March 1767   Recorded 12 March 1767

    Ref: Lunenburg County Deed Book 10, page 330

Note: Drury Warren (son of Thomas Warren) states in his ap-
      plication for a pension for his services in the Rev-
      olutionary War that he was born 26 December 1756 in
      Lunenburg County.
          That he moved to Henry County after the Revolu-
      tionary War, and then to Robertson County, State of
      Tennessee, in 1814.

WALL, John   Edgefield County, S. C.

    John Wall of Edgefield County, State of South Carolina,
to Charles Wade of Halifax County, State of Virginia .....
cons. 20 pounds specie ... 211 acres, more or less, on the
Dan River ... adjoining Boyd and Faulkner.
Dated 2 October 1800   Recorded 27 April 1801

    Ref: Halifax County Deed Book 18, page 552

WARREN, Marriott   Richmond County, Ga.

   Samuel H. Warren and Rebecca, his wife, David Abernathy
and Jane, his wife, of Mecklenburg County, State of Virginia
and Marriott Warren of Richmond County, State of Georgia,
cons. slave named Jack,..convey to Edward Nolley, Trustee,
for the children of James Harris, deceased, ... 280½ acres
in Mecklenburg County, State of Virginia... adjoining
William Gregory and others..
Dated 19 Sept. 1829   Recorded 2 Feb. 1830

      Ref: Mecklenburg County Deed Book 25, page 253

              WILL OF MARRIOTT WARREN, SENR.

NAMES: Wife - Mary Warren
       Children mentioned in will but not by name.
       Brother John Warren
       Children to be educated.
       Wife and children to live with her father, or with my
       brother John Warren.
Executors: Brother John Warren and friends Edward Holmes and
           James Reekes.
Dated 12 Dec. 1798   Recorded 14 Jan. 1799

      Ref: Mecklemburg County Will Book 4, page 85

      Inventory and appraisal of the estate of Marriott
Warren, deceased, returned to Court by Edward Holmes, Executor.   Recorded 10 June 1799

Note: The children of Marriott Warren, Senr., were Samuel
      Holmes Warren, Jane Warren and Marriott Warren, Junr.

M.B. 17 Dec. 1794 - Marriott Warren and Mary Holmes, dau. of
                    Samuel Holmes, Senr.
                    Surety: Benjamin Suggett
                    Consent: Samuel Holmes, Senr.

      Ref: ELLIOTT: Mecklenburg County Marriage Records,
                    1765-1810, page 129

M.B. 12 Dec. 1820 - Samuel H. Warren and Elizabeth Rebecca
                    Delony
                    Surety: Ludwell E. Jones
      Married 14 Dec. 1820 by the Rev. James Smith

M.B. 16 Feb. 1824 - David H. Abernathy and Jane Warren
                    Surety: Samuel H. Warren

      Ref: ELLIOTT: Mecklenburg County Marriage Records,
                    1811-1853, pages 9 and 179

                            122

WILL OF JOHN WARREN

NAMES: Wife - Sarah Warren
      Children - Elizabeth Warren, Marriott Warren, John
              Warren, William Warren and Thomas Warren
Executors: Father-in-law Thomas Marriott, wife Sarah Warren,
         brothers-in-law Mark Jackson and Gideon Harris
Dated 31 October 1779   Recorded 22 Nov. 1779

    Ref: Brunswick County Will Book 5, page 83

Note: There is no extant record of the marriage of John
      Warren and Sarah Marriott. Sarah (Marriott) Warren
      married (2) William Holmes.

M.B. 15 Jan. 1782 - William Holmes and Sarah Warren, widow
               of John Warren
               Surety: Sack Pennington

    Ref: Brunswick County Marriage Records, page 28

WILL OF BENJAMIN WARREN

NAMES: Wife - not named in will and evidently deceased
      Sons - John Warren, Benjamin Warren, Junr.
      Daughters - Martha Jackson, Rebecca Hyde, Hannah
              Ogburn, Rittah Harris, Elizabeth Lashly
      Mentions Edward Wilson, Junr., son of Edward Wilson,
      Senr.
Executors: Sons John Warren and Benjamin Warren
Dated 17 May 1778   Recorded 22 June 1778

    Ref: Brunswick County Will Book 5, page 18

M.B. 27 June 1770 - Gideon Harris and Rittah (Henrietta ?)
               Warren
               Surety: Edward Fisher
               Consent: Benjamin Warren
Note: Gideon Harris son of Nathan Harris

M.B. 25 Feb. 1771 - William Ogburn and Hannah Warren
               Surety: Benjamin Warren

    Ref: Brunswick County Marriage Records, page 9

WILL OF ALLEN WARREN

NAMES: Wife - not mentioned in will and evidently deceased.
      Son - Benjamin Warren
      Leaves entire estate to son Benjamin Warren
Executor: Son Benjamin Warren
Witnesses: Thomas Warren, John Warren and Thomas Barham

Dated 15 March 1737/38   Recorded 16 Jan. 1744

Ref: Surry County Will Book 9, page 488

WILL OF THOMAS MARRIOTT

NAMES: Wife - not named in will and deceased
       Son - Thomas Marriott
       Daughters - Sarah Holmes, Elizabeth Robertson,
                   Hannah Davis
       Grandchildren - Elizabeth Warren, Marriott Warren,
                       John Warren, William Warren, Thomas
                       Warren and Warren Holmes, children
       of my daughter Sarah Holmes
Executors: Son Thomas Marriott, William Holmes, Nathaniel
           Robertson and Randolph Davis
Dated 21 October 1785   Recorded 24 Aug. 1789

Ref: Brunswick County Will Book 5, page 316

M.B. 23 October 1769 - Nathaniel Robinson (Robertson) and
                       Eliza Merritt (Elizabeth Marriott)

Ref: William & Mary Qtly (1) Vol. XX, page 195

RABON, Richard et als   Granville County, N. C.

     Know all men by these presents that we, Richard Rabon,
John King and Robert King, all of the Province of North
Carolina and County of Granville, Planters, do by these presents appoint our trusty friend William Scoggin of the County of Brunswick, Colony of Virginia, our lawful attorney to
demand of and from Thomas Wise of the County of Brunswick a
tract of land known as the land where the said Thomas Wise
now lives containing 225 acres wich was patented in the name
of William Williams.
17 January 1760   Recorded 28 April 1760

Ref: Brunswick County Deed Book 6, page 509

VAUGHAN, Richard J.   Dyer County, Tenn.

     Know all men by these presents that I, Richard J.
Vaughan of the County of Dyer, State of Tennessee, do appoint my friend William Peterson my true and lawful attorney
to collect what belongs to me from the sale of the land of
my mother, Elizabeth Vaughan, now deceased.
Dated 22 May 1842   Recorded June Court 1842

Ref: Brunswick County Deed Book 32, page 428

WILLSON, Samuel   * Sullivan County, N. C.

     To all whom these presents come, Know ye that I, Samuel
Wilson of Sullivan County, State of North Carolina, have
appointed Elijah Graves of the County of Mecklenburg, State
of Virginia, my lawful attorney to give title to a tract of
land on the west side of Grassy Creek ... containing 250
acres ... adjoining lands of John McNeal, Francis Howard and
Jacob Royster ... being the land where James Hunt, Junr. now
lives, and my attorney is to act as fully as if I were present in person.
Dated 29 August 1783   Recorded 9 Sept. 1783

     Ref: Mecklenburg County Deed Book 6, page 345

* Sullivan County formed in 1779 from Washington District
  (or county), North Carolina, but now State of Tennessee.

WORKMAN, Peter   Rowan County, N. C.

     Peter Workman of Rowan County, State of North Carolina,
to Anthony Tittle of Henry County, State of Virginia .....
cons. 40 pounds ... 115 acres of land on the north fork of
Goblin Town Creek ... being formerly the land where George
Workman lived.
Dated 11 March 1799   Recorded 14 May 1799

     Ref: Henry County Deed Book 6, page 50

WRIGHT, Elizabeth   Rutherford County, Tenn.

     Know all men by these presents that I, Elizabeth Wright
of the County of Rutherford, State of Tennessee, daughter of
Robert Wright, deceased, do appoint my friend Joseph Pollard
of Rutherford County, State of Tennessee, my true and lawful
attorney to ask for and demand from William Hendrick, or
such others in Mecklenburg County, State of Virginia, any
money due me as a legal heir of Robert Wright, deceased, or
which is or may come into the hands of the executor or the
administrator of the said estate.
Dated 29 October 1829   Recorded 18 Jan. 1830

     Nancy Wright appeared in Court and stated that her dau-
ghter, Elizabeth Wright, was 21 years old and upward.
     Sworn to before me J. C. Mitchell, Justice of the Peace
this 29th day of October 1829.
                              /s/ J. C. Mitchell, J.P.

     Ref: Mecklenburg County Deed Book 24, page 69

                              125

M.B. 16 Nov. 1792 - Robert Wright and Nancy Wright
              Surety: Austin Wright
              Robert Wright of Brunswick County

    Ref: ELLIOTT: Mecklenburg County Marriage Records,
              1765-1810, page 136

WRIGHT, Wesley et als   Green County, Ohio

    Know all men by these presents that we, Wesley Wright
and Mary M. Wright, late Mary M. Pearson (Person), of Green
County, State of Ohio, have authorized, nominated, constituted and appointed Peter Pierson (Person) of Green County,
State of Ohio, aforesaid, our true and lawful attorney, for
us and in our names, to sell, convey by deed of General War-
ranty, or otherwise, as he may think fit, all such lands in
the State of Virginia, as they, or she the said Mary M.
Wright, late Mary M. Person, no^{w}is or hereafter may be entitled as one of the heirs of her father Littleberry Person,
deceased.
    And also, in our names, to give, execute and acknow-
ledge a sufficient deed, or deeds, of conveyance, and to
collect, sue for and recover all debts, dues and legacies
due us and in our names and for our use such sums as may be
due to us, the said Wesley and Mary M. Wright as the heirs
of Peter Thomas, lately deceased, grandfather of the said
Mary M. Wright, and to collect and transmit such sums to us
and further to transact all such businesss as if we were
present at the doing thereof.
Dated 21 August 1815   Recorded 22 April 1816

    Ref: Brunswick County Deed Book 23, page 145

Note: Littleberry Person died intestate and an inventory of
    his estate and an appraisal were recorded 27 Dec. 1808.

    Ref: Brunswick County Will Book 7, page 310

M.B. 20 December 1810 - Wesley Wright and Mary M. Person
              Surety: Drury Person

M.B. -- Nov. 1786 - Littleberry Person and Mary Thomas *

* Minister's return made by the Rev. Thomas Lundie.

    Ref: Brunswick County Marriage Records, pages 178-349

Peter, son of Peter Thomas and Elizabeth Thomas, born
    2 December 1734.

    Ref: Bristol Parish Register, page 376

WALL, Michael   **Lawrence County, Ala.**

Know all men by these presents that I, Michael Wall of
Lawrence County, State of Alabama, do constitute and appoint
James M. Wall of the said County of Lawrence, State of Alabama, my true and lawful attorney, for me and in my name, to
make a settlement with Walter Spratley and all other persons
having in their possession, as guardians, administrators or
executors, any part of the estate of Martha Birdsong, deceased, late of the County of Sussex, State of Virginia, my
wife Nancy M. Wall being a sister and an heir of the said
Martha Birdsong, deceased, and a sister of Mary Birdsong,
deceased, also. The said settlement to be made under the
terms of the will of George Birdsong, deceased, which is on
record in Sussex County, State of Virginia.
Dated 11 January 1830

23 February 1830 - This day received of William J. Cocke,
administrator of Mary A. Birdsong, deceased, the sum of $87.
00, it being in full (and includes a receipt of Michael Wall
for $260.53) both together being his full proportion of the
said estate, and likewise his proportion in full of what
Martha Birdsong would have been entitled to in settlement.
Witnesses: Wm. S. Jeffries
          Wilie F. Ellis   /s/ J. M. Wall, Attorney
                                             in fact for M. Wall
Recorded at Court 4 March 1830

     Ref: Sussex County Deed Book "P", page 483

WILLETT, Simeon P.   **Lauderdale County, Ala.**

Know all men by these presents that we, Simeon P. Willett and Julia Willett, formerly Julia Gilliam, both of the
County of Lauderdale, State of Alabama, have appointed John
Key of the County of Lauderdale and state aforesaid, our
true and lawful attorney to ask, demand and recover for us
all properties and money to which we have a legal right, or
an equitable right, by virtue of the last will and testament
of Molly, or Mary, Tucker, deceased, late of the State of
Virginia.
     And also our part of the estate of Thomas Gilliam, dec-
eased, late of the State of Virginia, which may be coming to
us in the right of the said Julia Willett who is one of the
heirs of the said Thomas Gilliam, deceased.
Dated 8 May 1829   Recorded 5 Nov. 1829

     Ref: Sussex County Deed Book "P", page 449

M.B. 10 April 1801 - Capt. Stith Tucker and Polly (Mary)
                     Gilliam, daughter of Thomas Gilliam *
                     Surety: John Gilliam

Ref: <u>Southampton County Marriage Records, page 144</u>

* The foregoing marriage record is listed for information
only, and there may be no connection. There does not ap-
pear to be any will or other record of the estate of
Thomas Gilliam in Sussex County.

<u>WINN, William</u>   <u>Laurens District, S. C.</u>

     Know all men by these presents that I, William Winn of
Laurens District, State of South Carolina, for divers good
causes and considerations, me thereunto moving, have made,
ordained, authorized, constituted and appointed Alexander
Winn of the County of Lunenburg, State of Virginia, my true
and lawful attorney, for me and in my name, to ask, demand
and receive all sums of money due to me, or coming to me,
in the State of Virginia.
<u>Dated 23 May 1811</u>   <u>Recorded 12 Dec. 1811</u>

     Ref: <u>Lunenburg County Deed Book 22, page 165</u>

<u>YOUNG, William</u> et als   <u>Warren County, Tenn.</u>

     Joshua Young and Nancy Young, his wife, Henry Harter
and Elizabeth Harter, his wife, all of Montgomery County,
State of Virginia, John Young of the State of Tennessee,
Isaac Young and Polly Young, his wife, William Young and
Jane Young, his wife, all of Warren County, State of Tennes-
see, David Young and Polly Young, his wife, Thomas Young and
Susanna Young, his wife, James Cannady and Sally Cannady,
his wife, all of Franklin County, State of Virginia, and
Mary Young, the widow of Peter Young, sell to Thomas Helm of
of Franklin County, State of Virginia ... cons. $1,500.00 ..
493 acres lying on both sides of Pigg River in Franklin
County.
<u>Dated 11 November 1829</u>   <u>Recorded 7 June 1830</u>

     Ref: <u>Franklin County Deed Book 13, page 29</u>

M.B. 14 Nov. 1798 - Joshua Young and Nancy Walker
                    Surety: John Walker

M.B. 4 June 1799 - Henry Harter and Elizabeth Young
                   Surety: Peter Young

M.B. 22 Feb. 1813 - James N. Cannady and Sarah Young, dau.
                    of Peter Young
                    Surety: Thomas Young

     Ref: <u>Franklin County Marriage Records</u>

128

Brown cont.
  George 44
  Henry 20,21
  James 20
  Jesse 121
  John 17
  Valentine 121
  William 20,21
Browne, Abba 21
  William 21
Bruce, James 111
Bugg, Agnes 78
  Anselm 77
  Samuel 78
  Sarah 78
  William H. 18
Bullock, William 63
Bumpass, Diggs 12
  Fanny 12
Burnett, James 64
  John 49,64
  Judith Beck 64
  Phillip 114
  Thomas 47
Burrus, Henry C. 35
Burt, Matthew 101
Burton, John 98,102
Burwell, Lewis 57,58
  Thacker 72
Bush, Thomas 108
Butler, James 24
  Winifred 22,25
Bynum, Britain 56
  Francis 56

Cain, Thomas 56
Call, William 87
Campbell, Bersheba 83
  Rebecca 83
Cannady, James 128
  Sally 128
Cardwell, Daniel 26
  George 26
  John 26
  Maryann 26
  Mary Ann 26
  Obedience 26
  Peter 26
  Richard 26,27
  Susanna 26
  Susannah 26
  Thomas, Sr. 26
  Thomas 26
  Thomas Perrin 26
Carleton, John Hyde 59
  Thomas 54
Carrington, Clement 11
Carter, John 14,15
  Polly 14
  Theoderick 36
  Thomas 14,15,98
  Tyree 110
Cato, Dixon 114
  Martha 56
  Robert 114
  Rolling 114
  Sally 114
  Wiley 114
  William 114
Chaffin, Thomas 101
Chandler, Joel 77,78
Chapman, Alexander 34
Chappell, James 28
  Martha 28
Cheatham, Abraham 33
  Ann 32,33
  Daniel 119
  Edward 33
  Elizabeth 32,33
  Elizabeth, Jr. 33
  James 32,33
  Joseph 16
  Leonard 32,33
  Leonard, Jr. 33

Cheatham cont.
  Obadiah 119
  Phebe 119
  Tabitha 33
Cheek, Robert 23
Childress, John 47
Chisolm, Obadiah 26
Chiswell, James 47
Chitwood, John 80
  Sally 80
Chrisman, Polly 114
  William 114
Christopher, Elizabeth 50
  William 50
Clanton, George 104
Clark, Caroline M.
  Caroline Matilda 31
  Isham 31
  Joseph 31
  Nancy 31
  Penelope 26
  Phebe 31
  Silas 31
Clarke, Archibald 66
Clausel, Alexander 96
  Clausel 60,82,96,97
  Clausel B. 73
  Joseph B. 68,82,100
  Richard 97
  Richard, Jr. 82
  Richard W. 51
  Sally S. 96
  Susanna 96
Clay, Eleazar 34,36
  Henry 71
  James, Sr. 34,36
  James 34
  Jeremiah 36
  John 35
  Loury 74
  Lucy Green 71
  Margaret 34
  Patsy 35
  Patsy Ingram 35
  Phebe 33
  Rebecca 50
  William 74
Clayton, Alexander 16
  Elizabeth 16
  Sally 16
  John 16
Clements, Christopher 27
  William 27
  William R. B. 27
Cocke, Abraham 47
  Elizabeth 89
  James 89
  William J. 127
Coleman, Cluverius 58
  Mary Ligon 34
Coles, Isaac 84
Collier, John C. 27
  Sylvia 114
Collins, Elisha 110
  James 110
  John 42,43,110
  John, Jr. 110
  Joseph 110
  Nancy 110
  Peter 110
  William 110
Cook, Benjamin 37
  Foster 113
  John 67
  Joseph 37
Cooper, James 118
  Joseph 105
  Mary 83
Coppage, Charles 24
Cousins, Peter 36
Cowan, Mary 46
  William 46
Cowen, David 33
Cox, Edith 118

Cox cont.
  Edward 87
  John, Jr. 89
Creath, Rev. William 49,
    96,119
  William 39
Crenshaw, Gideon 56
Crowder, Godfrey 28,29,33,
    68
  John 39
  Nancy 29
  Sterling 22
Cunningham, Alice 68
  Eliza F. 37
  James 68,69
  John 13
  Robert F. 37
Cyer, Benjamin 29

Dabbs, Rev. Richard 116
  Rev. Richard, Jr. 16
Dailey, Edmund 38
Daley, Ambrose 28
  Josiah 28
Daniel, Elizabeth 98
  Hezekiah 93
  Josiah 98
Davis, Elizabeth 29
  Eliza H. 115
  Hannah 124
  Jane 115
  John 115
  John, Jr. 14,49
  Joshua 41
  Nancy 41
  Randolph 124
  Unity C. 115
  William 14,22,49
DeGraffenreid, Tscharher
    46,47
Delony, Elizabeth Rebecca
    122
  Henry 87
Dillon, Elizabeth 43
  Henry 42
  Thomas 34
Dixon, Agnes 94
  Edmund 38
  Jacob 94
  Joyce 38
  Sanford 94
  Warren 38
  William, Sr. 38
  William 38,94
  William, Jr. 38
Dobie, William 19
Dobson, Joseph 87
  Rev. Thomas 50
Dodson, Edward 60
  George, Sr. 79
  Margaret 79
  Rosannah 79
  William 49,60
Donald, Alexander 57
Dorr, Alexander 108
Dortch, Jesse 41
Doub, John, Jr. 96
Douglas, William 109
Draper, Asa 40
  Elizabeth 39,40
  Frances 40
  John 40
  John Wesley 40
  Martin 40
  Solomon 39,97
  Solomon, Jr. 39,40
  Thomas 40
  William 39,40
  William, Jr. 40
Drury, Richard 62
Dunnington, Polly 41
  Reuben 41
Dupree, Moses A. 100
Dyer, David 37

Griffin cont.
Ralph 54
Sarah 53,54
Susannah 54
Grizzard, William 62,63
Gunston, Mary 108

Haggard, French 47
Haile, Leeman 55
Thomas 55
Hailey, Jane 54
John 55
Phillip R. 29
Thomas 53,54,55
William 77
Hairston, Robert 29
Haldane, James 9
Hale, Rittah 30
Hales, Robert 17
Haley, James 67
Hall, Anne 87
James 17,28,87
Miles 72
Sally 17
Hamblin, Charles 53
Hamilton, Joseph 59
Hamlett, James 11,12
Hamlin, Charles 53
Hammond, John 39 -
Hancock, Douglas 61
George 71
Martin 61
Sarah 61
Hanserd, Richard 65
Sarah 65
Hardiman, Constant 84
Harper, Benjamin 112
Benjamin I. 112
Elizabeth 59
Howell P. 27
Harris, Charles 112
Gideon 123
James 122
Jonathon 17
Nathan 123
Rittah 123
Sterling 9
Sylvia 9
Sylvania Lane 9
William 36
Harrison, Footman 82
Lovell 83
Thomas 23
Hart, Beasley 16
Richard 16
Reuben 16
Thomas 16
William 16
Harter, Elizabeth 128
Henry 128
Harvey, Blasinghame 61
Druscilla 61
Francis 61
John 61
Molly 61
Nathan 61
Sally 61
Thomas, Sr. 61
Thomas 61
William 61
Harwell, Grief 23,25
James 23,25,49
Vines 112
Haskins, Christopher 14,
18
Creed 74
Edward 72
Robert 70
Susanna 51
Hatchell, Sally 18
Hatchett, Archibald 101
Jane 101
John 101
Thomas 101

Hatchett cont.
William 101,102,103
Hauser, George 96
Hawkins, William 47
Hay, Balaam 62,63,64
Edith, Sr. 63
Edith 62,63
Edith, Jr. 62,63
Frances 63
Icy 63
John 63
Lucy 62,63
Richard, Sr. 63
Richard 62,63
Richard, Jr. 62,63
Sealah 62,63
Sealy 62
Hayes, Henry 9
Thomas 82
W. 82
William 82
Haynes, Parmenas 76
Richard 76
Heath, Joseph, Jr. 76
William 76
Helm, Thomas 128
Hendrick, William 14,99,
115,125
Henry, John 97
Herndon, Jane 103
Joseph 103
Sallie 103
Hester, Anna 88
James 55,88,92
Martha 92
Nancy 70
Robert 69,70
Samuel 80
Hewell, Joseph, Jr. 90
Hightower, George 117
Joshua 117
Susannah 116
William 116
Hill, Ann 54
Elizabeth 54
Elizabeth Gold 54
James 54
Mary 11
Thomas 10
Hillhouse, John 21
Hine, Calvin 75
Hix, Amey 77
Nathaniel 78
Sally 110
Sarah 77
Hobbs, Hamilton 63
Hoggis, Fleman 108
John 108
Holland, Jonas M. 64
Theodosia 64
Holloway, Ann 87
Bennett 86,87
Dianna 87
Diannah 87
George 85,86,87
James 85,86,87
John 85,86,87
Sarah 86
Thomas 87
William 86,87
Holmes, David 58
Edward 122
John 58
Martha 78
Mary 122
Patty 78
Samuel, Sr. 122
Sarah 124
Warren 124
William 123,124
Holt, John 11,20
William 10
Hopkins, Samuel 48,77,99
Samuel, Jr. 99

Howard, Francis 125
Howerton, Richard 65
Hubbard, Samuel 43
Hudson, John 58
Taffanus 29
Hulet, William 84
Humphreys, Henry 94
Hunt, James, Jr. 125
John 105
Ruth 105
Hutcheson, David C. 27
John 64
Nancy 119
Peter, Sr. 51
Hutchins, Winifred 83
Hutt, Daniel 57
Hyde, Elinor 59
Elizabeth 59
Irvin 59
James 59
John, Sr. 59
John 39
John, Jr. 59
Rebecca 123
Robert 59,60
Thomas 59

Ingram, Elizabeth   118
John 35,112
Mary Ann 112
Moses 35
Patsy 35
Patty 35
Robert 118
Thomas 35,112

Jackson, Francis 26
Joel 103
Mark 123
Martha 123
James, John 120
Jeffries, William S. 127
Jenings, Elizabeth 61
Pleasant 61
Robert 61
Jeter, Lucy 65
William 47
Johns, John 66
Johnson, Benjamin 67
Caleb 60,69
Daniel 67
Elizabeth 14
John 14,67
John R. 67
Josiah 115
Miles 98
Johnston, Caleb 60
Lucy 60
Samuel 67
Thomas Rev. 11,115
Joiner, Elizabeth 83
Jones, Caroline 95
Daniel 102,109
David 109
Edward 60,95
Edward, Jr. 95
Elizabeth 94,95
Elizabeth R. 95
Frederick 24,25
Harwood 89
James 17,95
Jane 109
Job 109
John, Sr. 109
John 94,109
John J. 75
Joseph 90
Lucy 68
Ludwell E. 122
Margaret 109
Maria 95
Mary 17
Nancy 95
Penelope 22,25

134

Powell cont.
  William H. 63
P'Pool, Stephen 51,89
Presson, Nicholas 19,20
Price, Anne 38
  Evan 80
  Jonathon 80
  Randolph 100
  William 38
Pride, John, Jr. 73
Proctor, Joshua 67
  Thomas 107
Pruett, Anthony 52
Pruit, Elizabeth 94
  Samuel 94
Prunty, Robert 120
Pryor, Luke 9
Pulliam, Benjamin 114
  Elizabeth 33
Puryear, Elijah 30,53,88,
  92
  Elizabeth 68
  Elizabeth P. 69
  Hezekiah 95,96,97
  Jane 50
  John, Sr. 96,97
  John 50,96
  John, Jr. 96,97
  John III 97
  Martha 96,97
  Mary 97
  Rebekah 95
  Reuben 51,97
  Richard Clausel 96
  Sally S. 96
  Samuel 96,97
  Sarah 97
  Seymour 97
  Thomas 37,68,69
  William 97
Putney, Anthony 94
  Eliza 93

Rabon, Richard 124
Ragland, John, Sr. 111
Ragsdale, John 47,60
  Rachel 60
  Robert 60
Rainey, Frederick 23
  Mat 76
Ramsey, John 120,121
Read, Clement, Sr. 11
  Clement, Jr. 11,12
  Isaac 11
  James Rev. 40,65,69
  M. 11
  Mary Hill 11
  Mary Nash 11
  Thomas Col. 12,66
  Thomas 11
  William 102
Rear, Joseph 21
Reed, William 82
Reekes, James 122
Reese, Edward 83
Renn, Joseph 83
Rice, Holeman 40,65
Richards, Rev. William 68,
  69,88,95
Richardson, Conrad 115
  Elizabeth 18,115
  George 99
  Holt 85
Rives, Edward 99
  Joana 98
  John 99
  Mary 99
  Peter 63
  Robert 99
  Robert C. 63
  Thomas 98
  William 98
Roach, Cuthbert 95
Robards, John 72,73

Robards cont.
  Sarah 73
  William 73
Roberson, James 100
  Patsy 100
Roberts, Alexander 102
  Anselm 18
  Bartholomew 101
  Bartlett 101,102,103
  Francis, Sr. 102
  Francis 101,103
  Francis, Jr. 101,102,
    103
  Hannah 102
  Jane 103
  Jesse 104
  John 100,101,102,103
  Martha 101,103
  Mary 102
  Naaman 96
  Nancy 18
  Nancy Bottom 18
  Prudence 101,102,103
  Rebecca 101
  Susanna 100,101
  Thomas, Sr. 102
  Thomas 49,100,101,102,
    103
  Thomas Jr. 102
Robertson, Elizabeth 124
  Henry 60
  John 56
  Nathaniel 124
  Robert W. 99
Robinson, John 23,93,98,
  113
  Sally 99
Roffe, Susanna 119
Rodger, Robert R. 37
Rogers, George 116
Rooks, Buckner 94
  Fanny 94
Rose, William 13
Rowland, Rachel 60
  Richard 60
Royster, Abel 40
  Charles M. 53
  Clarke 66
  Elizabeth 39,40
  Frances 39
  Granderson 40
  Hardy 40
  Harrison 40
  Henry 40
  Jacob 125
  John 40
  Joseph 40
  Lucy 65
  Solomon 40
  William 40
Rucker, James 12
  Lucy L. 12
  Lucy LeGrand 12
Rudd, Elizabeth 117
  Joseph 56,96
  Thomas 118
  Wilmoth 56
Russell, Benjamin B. 15
  James T. 115
  Richard 21

Sandifer, John 34
Sargeant, Elizabeth 53
  William 53
Saunders, Rev. Hubbard 9
Saylor, Alexander 58
Scoggin, William 124
Scott, Rev. Thomas 27
Seaborn, Howell 63
  Louisa 62
Sears, Milley 20
Seat, Josiah 53
  Margaret 53
Seay, John 81

Seay cont.
  Sarah 81
Sharp, John 79
  Robert 79
Shelburne, James Rev. 119
  Mary 119
Shell, Betsy 104
  Byron 104
  Edmund 9
  Lemon 104
  Stephen 104
  William, Sr. 104
  William 104
Shelton, James 68,69
  Nancy 68,69
Sills, William 62
Simmons, Benjamin 105
  John 31
  Phebe 31
  Sally 105
Sims, Frederick 106
Skinker, John 83
Slate, Caroline Matilda 31
  William 31
Slause, Agnes 79
Smith, Buckner 55
  Elizabeth 55
  Frances 31
  Ichabod 117
  James, Sr. 107
  James Rev. 122
  James 31,107
  John 23,24,118
  John P. 107
  Nancy 31
  Paulina 117
  Samuel 39
  Samuel Henry 107
  William F. 107
Smithson, Ann 117
  Betty 52
  James A. 52
  John 118
Spain, Claiborne 91
  Frances 91
  Susanna 107
Speed, Elizabeth 65
  Elizabeth J. 33
  Elizabeth Julia 33
  Henry 33,65
  John 65,87,106
  John, Jr. 65
  John, son of Lewis 65
  Joseph 27,65,106
  Joseph, Jr. 65
  Lewis 65
  Martha 65
  Mary 65
  Mathias 65
  Mathias, son of Lewis 65
  Polly 33
  Sarah 65,106
  Will James 65
Spratley, Walter 127
Stanfield, Thomas 92
Starling, William 108
Steel, William 108
Stephens, Debby 14
  Deborah, Jr. 14,15
  Hailey 14
  Haley 14
  John 14
  Joseph 14
  Joshua 14,15
  Thomas 13,14
Stevens, Deborah 14,15
  John 14
  Mary 13,14
  Polly 15
  Thomas 14,15
Stewart, Nevin 58
  Reuben 96
Stith, Buckner 107
  Drury 106

Stith cont.
  Richard 59
Stokes, H. F. 95
Stone, Asher 119
  Daniel 120
  Hannah 120
  Hannah Love 116
  Isaac 119
  Lucy 70
  Marvel 51
  Nancy H. 120
  Richard 37
  Sally 116
  Samuel 119
  Stephen 51
  Tabitha 119
  William 116,119,120
  William, Jr. 119
Stovall, Elizabeth 105
  George 105
  John 106
  Joseph 105
  Pleasant 105
  Ruth 105
  Thomas 105
Sturdivant, Jemima 91
Suggett, Benjamin 122
Sullivant, John 12
  Lucas 48
Swepson, Richard 32
  William M. 60

Tabb, Edward L. 86
Talliaferro, Richard 47
Tanner, Branch 103
  Matthew 56
Tarry, George 99
Tarwater, George T. 106
Taylor, Benjamin 114
  Daniel 105
  Drury 109
  Edmund 23
  Howell 77,78
  James 105
  James, Jr. 49
  Joseph 71
  Nancy 110
  Polly 114
  Sarah 109
  William 77,78,110
Tedford, Margaret 79
Terry, Nathaniel 111
Thomas, David 22,23,24,25,
  104
  David W. 22
  Elizabeth 126
  Mary 126
  Peter 126
  Phillip 36
  Rebecca 25
  Rebekah 22
Thompson, Harmon 67
Thornton, Susannah 61
  William 61
Threewits, Ann 91
  Frances 91
  Frederick 91
  Peter 91
Thweatt, Drury 112
  William 101,112
Tillotson, Edward 55
  William 55
Tittle, Anthony 125
Tomlinson, John 83
Toone, Thomas 21
Torian, George 111
  Jacob 111
  Martha 111
  Mary 111
  Nancy, Sr. 111
  Obedience 111
  Peter, Sr. 111
  Polly 111
  Scare 111

Torian cont.
  Thomas 111
Towler, Jechonias 47
Townes, Elizabeth 79
  Henry 79
Troy, Matthew 45
Tuck, Bennet 60
Tucker, Hartwell 112
  James 39
  Mary 127
  Mary Ann 112
  Molly 127
  Sterling 112
  Stith Capt. 127
  William 108,120
  Wright Rev. 112
Turbyfield, Rebecca 59
Turner, John 109
  Mary 98
  Matthew 116
  Nancy 116
  Sugars, Jr. 56
  Terisha 98
  Stephen 98
  William 92,109

Underdown, Betty 61

Vaughan, Ambrose 45
  Elizabeth 124
  James 77
  Reuben 65
  Richard 45
  Richard J. 124
  William 77
Vincent, Ann 113,114
  Henry 113
  Joshua 113
  Peter 113
  Rebekah 113
  Thomas 113

Wade, Charles 121
  Hampton 81
  Robert, Sr. 116
Waddill, Frances 52
  John 66
  Noel 52
  Pleasant 66
  William 52
Walden, Sarah 59
Walker, Ann 118
  Aurelius 116,117
  Benjamin 116,117
  David 100
  Elizabeth 118
  George Hightower 116,117
  Geo. Hightower 119
  John 82,128
  John C. 21
  Mary 119
  Matthew 116
  Molly 119
  Nancy 128
  Nancy Turner 116
  Paulina 118
  Sally 116,119
  Susannah 117,118
  Sylvanus, Sr. 118
  Sylvanus 116
  Tandy 117
  William 117
Wall, J. M. 127
  James M. 127
  John 121
  Michael 127
  Nancy M. 127
  William C. 51
Waller, John 32
Walton, Edward 97
  Robert 12
  Sherwood 12
Warden, Thomas 121
Warren, Allen 123

Warren cont.
  Ambrose 120
  Benjamin 123
  Benjamin, Jr. 123
  Benjamin H. 15
  Drury 120,121
  Elijah 120
  Elizabeth 123,124
  Hannah 123
  Jane 120,122
  John 122,123,124
  Marriott, Sr. 122
  Marriott 122,123,124
  Mary 122
  Nancy 120
  Rebecca 122
  Rittah 123
  Robert H. 46
  Samuel H. 15,122
  Sarah 123
  Thomas 120,121,123,124
  William 120,123,124
  Zachariah 120
Watkins, Daniel D. 69
  Edward 74
  Frederick 73
  James 52
  Joel 21
  John 19
  William Durham 92
Weakley, Jane 108
  Robert 108
  Samuel 108
Weatherford, Rev. John 61
Webb, John 23
  Thomas 45
Weeks, John 105
Wells, Matthew 67
West, Robert 27
White, B(lumer) 24
  Burgess 24,25
  Elisha 21
  James 19
  John 61
  Mary 22
  Sarah 22,25
  William 61,62
Wilborn, Rebecca 75
Wilborne, Betsy 75
  William 75
Wilburn, Benjamin O. 90
  Henry H. 75
  James 75
  John K. 75
  Rebecca 75
  William 75
Wilkerson, David 94
  Major 77
  Martha 94
  Sarah 94
  William 94
Wilkes, Burwell 9
Wilkins, James 55,77
  Sarah 55
  Thomas 29
Wilkinson, Martha 93
Willett, Julia 127
  Simeon P. 127
Williams, Drury 72
  John Rev. 51,69,101
  John 12,35
  Lazarus 47
  Lewis, Jr. 35
  Parmenas 98
  Robert 102
  Samuel 111
  William 30,38,124
Williamson, Geo. 72
  Joseph 94
  Robert 80
Willingham, Jeremiah 50
  Rebeccah 50
Willis, Lucy 29
  Richard 39

Wilson, Ann 32
  Daniel, Sr. 33
  Daniel 33,102
  Edward 123
  Edward, Jr. 123
  Hannah 119
  Henry 13,27
  James 33,64,68,73,85
  John 32,33,50,58,69
  John, Jr. 33
  Lucy 33,73
  Miles 33
  Robert 17,54,120
  Robert B. 119
  Samuel 125
  Sarah 54
  Tabitha 33
  Tabitha, Jr. 33
  Thomas 33
  Uel 33
Winckler, John 18
Winfrey, David 94
Winkler, John 47
Winn, Alexander 128
  Richard 72
  William 128
Wise, Thomas 124
Wood, Elizabeth 57,58
  John 115
  William 57,58
Wooding, Martha 28
  Robert 28
  Thomas H. 28
Woodson, David 45
Wooten, Edward 20
  Sylvia 20
Wooton, Martha 59
Wootton, Edward, Sr. 20
  Edward 19,20
  Edward, Jr. 20
  Eldridge 19
  George 19
  Miranda 19
Workman, George 125
  Peter 125
Worsham, John 66
  Polly 66
  Thomas 71
Wortham, Thomas P. 115
Wrenn, Jesse 17
  Nathan 17
Wright, Austin 126
  Elizabeth 125
  John 41,49
  John M. 115
  Joshua 41
  Mary M. 126
  Nancy 41,49,125,126
  Polly 41
  Reuben 41,115
  Reuben, Jr. 41
  Robert 41,125,126
  Stephen P. H. 115
  Thomas 41
  Unity C. 115
  Wesley 126
  William 41
Wyche, Henry, Jr. 113
  Nathaniel 62
Wyatt, Henry 29
  Susanna 29
Wynn, Kitty 65

Yancey, Dolly 88
  Mary 88
  Zachariah 54
Young, David 128
  Elizabeth 128
  Isaac 128
  James 23
  Jane 128
  John 128
  Joshua 128
  Mary 128

Young cont.
  Michael 23
  Nancy 128
  Peter 128
  Polly 128
  Sarah 128
  Susanna 128
  Thomas 128
  William 128

www.ingramcontent.com/pod-product-compliance
Lightning Source LLC
Chambersburg PA
CBHW021832020426
42334CB00014B/597